PEOPLE
OF THE
COVENANT

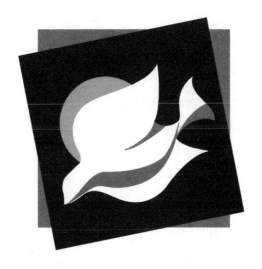

JACK W. HAYFORD
Executive Editor

THOMAS NELSON
Since 1798

NASHVILLE   DALLAS   MEXICO CITY   RIO DE JANEIRO

Published in Nashville, Tennessee, by Thomas Nelson. Thomas Nelson is a registered trademark of Thomas Nelson, Inc.

Thomas Nelson, Inc., titles may be purchased in bulk for educational, business, fund-raising, or sales promotional use. For information, please e-mail SpecialMarkets@ThomasNelson.com.

Unless otherwise indicated, all Scripture quotations are from the New King James Version, copyright ©1979, 1980, 1982, 1990, 2004 by Thomas Nelson Inc.

Hayford, Jack W.

People of the Covenant

ISBN-13: 978-1-4185-4860-5

Printed in the United States of America

11 12 13 14 15 [QG] 6 5 4 3 2 1

TABLE OF CONTENTS

PREFACE

The Blood and the Word

In this study, you will discover how far God's thoughts exceed even the very best ideas the world can offer. We will explore the importance of the blood of Jesus in everyday living and the power of the Covenant sealed by the blood of our Lord.

We are people of the Covenant. This Covenant is characterized by *both* blood and a book—the blood of Jesus Christ and the Word of the living God. Both are cleansing agents. Both are weapons to be wielded in our spiritual conflict with darkness. Both are connected in at least three other ways:

1. The *scrolls* and the mercy seat were sprinkled with *blood* (Hebrews 9:19, 21).
2. *Blood* flowed from *Jesus'* side. Jesus is God's Word made flesh (John 1:14; 19:34).
3. Our Lord's communion table is prepared with both *wine* and *bread* (Matthew 4:4; 26:26–28; John 6:32–58; 1 Corinthians 11:24, 25).

As you study the thirteen lessons in this book, you'll discover:
Concerning the BLOOD

- God is a God who makes covenants—blood-sealed covenants—for the purpose of establishing a right relationship with us, His children. God, who is perfect and true, has revealed Himself in His Word, the Bible, which is perfect and true (Session 1).
- Jesus Himself is the ultimate, once-for-all, blood Sacrifice who has opened the way to boldly approach Father God and confidently live in the power of the Holy Spirit (Session 5).
- The blood of Jesus the Lamb of God is also powerful. It protects us, purges us, and pulverizes Satan, our enemy (Session 7).
- The blood of Jesus cleanses us, giving us a clear conscience and a love for others (Session 8).

Concerning the WORD

- The Bible not only measures our lives and our words, but it also shows us how to live and speak (Session 2).
- The Author of the Bible makes His Word both powerful and practical. It applies to all aspects of life (Session 6).
- The Word of God is like food to be eaten or seed to be sown, bringing growth and yielding harvest (Session 9).
- God's promises are "exceedingly great and precious" (Session 11).

Concerning both the BLOOD and the WORD

- Our disobedience created a need not only for our tracks to be covered, but for us to be covered (Session. 3).
- Abel believed God's Word and obediently brought a blood offering to the Lord (Session 4).
- Communion is more than a sacrament (Session 10).
- Revelation 12:11 says that believers overcome their adversary "by the blood of the Lamb and by the word of their testimony" (Session 12).
- Living with Christ's return in view brings great hope and purpose to the present (Conclusion).

Keys of the Kingdom

KEYS CAN BE SYMBOLS of possession, of the right and ability to acquire, clarify, open or ignite. Keys can be concepts that unleash mind-boggling possibilities. Keys clear the way to a possibility otherwise obstructed!

Jesus spoke of keys: "And I will give you the keys of the kingdom of heaven, and whatever you bind on earth will be bound in heaven, and whatever you loose on earth will be loosed in heaven" (Matthew. 16:19).

While Jesus did not define the "keys" He has given, it is clear that He did confer specific tools upon His church which grant us access to a realm of spiritual "partnership" with Him. The "keys" are concepts or biblical themes, traceable throughout Scripture, which are verifiably dynamic when applied with solid faith under the lordship of Jesus Christ. The "partnership" is the essential feature of this enabling grace; allowing believers to receive Christ's promise of "kingdom keys," and to be assured of the Holy Spirit's readiness to actuate their power in the life of the believer.

Faithful students of the Word of God, and some of today's most respected Christian leaders, have noted some of the primary themes which undergird this spiritual partnership. A concise presentation of many of these primary themes can be found in the Kingdom Dynamics feature of *The New Spirit-Filled Life Bible*. The *New Spirit-Filled Life Study Guide Series*, an outgrowth of this Kingdom Dynamics feature, provides a treasury of more in-depth insights on these central truths. This study series offers challenges and insights designed to enable you to more readily understand and appropriate certain dynamic "Kingdom Keys."

Each study guide has twelve to fourteen lessons, and a number of helpful features have been developed to assist you in your study, each marked by a symbol and heading for easy identification.

 ## Kingdom Key

KINGDOM KEY identifies the foundational Scripture passage for each study session and highlights a basic concept or principle presented in the text along with cross-referenced passages.

Kingdom Life

The KINGDOM LIFE feature is designed to give practical understanding and insight. This feature will assist you in comprehending the truths contained in Scripture and applying them to your day-to-day needs, hurts, relationships, concerns, or circumstances.

Word Wealth

The WORD WEALTH feature provides important definitions of key terms.

Behind the Scenes

BEHIND THE SCENES supplies information about cultural beliefs and practices, doctrinal disputes, and various types of background information that will illuminate Bible passages and teachings.

Kingdom Extra

The optional KINGDOM EXTRA feature will guide you to Bible dictionaries, Bible encyclopedias, and other resources that will enable you to gain further insight into a given topic.

Probing the Depths

Finally, PROBING THE DEPTHS will present any controversial issues raised by particular lessons and may cite Bible passages or other sources to assist you in arriving at your own conclusions.

This Spirit-Filled Life Study Guide is a comprehensive resource presenting study and life-application questions and exercises with spaces provided to record your answers. These study guides are designed to provide all you need to gain a good, basic understanding of the covered theme and apply biblical counsel to your life. You will need only a heart and mind open to the Holy Spirit, a prayerful attitude, a pencil and a Bible to complete the studies and apply the truths they contain. However, you may want to have a notebook handy if you plan to expand your study to include the optional Kingdom Extra feature.

The Bible study method used in this series employs four basic steps:

1. *Observation:* What does the text say?
2. *Interpretation:* What is the original meaning of the text?
3. *Correlation:* What light can be shed on this text by other Scripture passages?
4. *Application:* How should my life change in response to the Holy Spirit's teaching of this text?

The New King James Version is the translation used wherever Scripture portions are cited in the *New Spirit-Filled Life Study Guide* series. Using this translation with this series will make your study easier, but it is certainly not imperative, and you will profit through use of any translation you choose.

Through Bible study, you will grow in your essential understanding of the Lord, His kingdom and your place in it; but you need more. The Holy Spirit was sent to teach us "all things" (John 14:26; 1 Corinthians 2:13). Rely on the Holy Spirit to guide your study and your application of the Bible's truths. Bathe your study time in prayer as you use this series to learn of Him and His plan for your life. Ask the Spirit of God to illuminate the text, enlighten your mind, humble your will, and comfort your heart. And as you explore the Word of God and find the keys to unlock its riches, may the Holy Spirit fill every fiber of your being with the joy and power God longs to give all His children. Read diligently on. Stay open and submissive to Him. Learn to live your life as the Creator intended. You will not be disappointed. He promises you!

SESSION ONE

The Blood of the Covenant

Ephesians 2:13 But now in Christ Jesus you who once were far off have been brought near by the blood of Christ.

It is important that, as believers in Jesus Christ, we fully understand what the Bible teaches about the blood of the covenant. We live in an age of cultural relativism. The truth that God has structured the universe in such a way that we can only come to Him through the blood of Jesus Christ is difficult to understand. In fact, to many in our society who believe that they are enlightened or even on a higher plane of consciousness, Christianity is viewed as some kind of primitive, blood-stained religion. The question is constantly raised, "Why can't I come to God my own way? Why do I need to accept Jesus Christ?" The truth—that it is only through the death and resurrection of Christ and through the shedding of His blood that we can be cleansed of our sins—is not only misunderstood, but challenged.

In understanding the blood of the covenant, the key question must be asked: Why is it only through the blood that my sins can be forgiven?

Read: Hebrews 9:1–28

Questions:

What is your current understanding of covenant and its implications?

✎ _____

_____

_____

What is your current understanding of Hebrews 9:22—"And according to the law almost all things are purified with blood, and without shedding of blood there is no remission"?

✎ _____

_____

_____

Word Wealth—*Covenant*

Covenant, *berit* (beh-reet'); Strong's #1285: A covenant, compact, pledge, treaty, agreement. This is one of the most theologically important words in the Bible, appearing more than 250 times in the Old Testament. A *berit* may be made between a king and his people or by God with His people.

Kingdom Life—*God is the Covenant Maker*

As we read through the Bible, it is amazing to see the continuity of thought from Genesis to Revelation. It is like one enormous tapestry woven by a Master Artist whose thousands of threads come together in an incredibly intricate design of color and patterns. The Bible has specific themes that are developed and carried through perfectly by different men and women over centuries. One such key theme in Scripture is the concept that God is a covenant maker.

We read in Genesis 1:3–5: "Then God said, 'Let there be light'; and there was light. And God saw the light, that it was good; and God divided the light from the darkness. God called the light Day, and the darkness He called Night. So the evening and the morning were the first day."

At the very beginning of Creation, God reveals Himself as the Covenant Maker. For further understanding of this idea of God's activity in Creation as acts of covenant, read Jeremiah 33:20–21.

Read: Genesis 9:1–17

Questions:

How would you define the word "covenant?"

_____

_____

_____

What covenants exist in our society?

_____

_____

_____

It is obvious that covenants in our society are not taken as seriously as in biblical days. Why do you believe this is so?

_____

_____

_____

Kingdom Extra

Read Genesis 15:1–21.

The direct requirement of a blood sacrifice as the means of establishing covenant first appears in this episode (vv. 1–21) and in God's instruction to Abraham. The animals to be offered were selected, cut in halves, and arranged in proper order opposite one another. In subsequent covenants, the covenant parties then passed between the halves indicating that they were irrevocably bound together in blood. The cutting in halves of the sacrifice spoke of the end of existing lives for the sake of establishing a new bond or covenant. The sacred nature of this bond was attested to by the shedding of lifeblood. In this instance, only God passed between the pieces, indicating that it was His covenant and He would assume responsibility for its administration. Present in this account of covenant-making are three essential ingredients: 1) a bond that originates from God's initiative, 2) the offering of a blood sacrifice as a requirement of covenant, and 3) God's sovereign administration of the outcome of His oath.

In Genesis 15:10, we learn that God is not only the God of the covenant, but that He is the author of a specific kind of covenant—the blood covenant.

 ## Kingdom Life—*Atonement*

In Leviticus 17:11 we learn of the power of the blood. Scripture clearly points out, "It is the blood that makes atonement for the soul." The idea of a blood sacrifice appears about sixty times in the Book of Leviticus.

The truth that God is a covenant maker who restores us to a right relationship with Him through the blood of the covenant is central to the Bible. Thus, religions that teach one can have a relationship with God apart from the blood of the covenant must be false. Hinduism and Buddhism teach that man and God can have a relationship through man's good works. Yet the Bible teaches that man and God can only come together through the blood of the covenant, which culminates in the death and resurrection of Jesus Christ—the blood of the Lamb.

Read: Exodus 12:12–13; John 1:29; Galatians 1:4; Hebrews 9:22

Questions:

John called Jesus "the Lamb of God." What is your understanding of this title?

It has been said the meaning of "atonement" can be found by dividing the syllables in this way: at-one-ment. What insight can you gain about the meaning of the word from this technique?

✎ _____

_____

Jesus willingly gave His life as the Lamb of God. In what way does this reveal God's desire for "at-one-ment" with you?

✎ _____

_____

Probing the Depths

Read Leviticus 17:11.

This verse is the clearest statement in Scripture of the necessity of blood as it relates to sacrificial offerings: "the life . . . is in the blood." Life and blood were given upon the altar for a specific purpose of making atonement, or attaining reconciliation with God. Apart from the shedding of blood or giving of a life, there was no atonement. This established ordinance is reaffirmed in the New Covenant (the Covenant sealed by the blood of Christ) in Hebrews 9:22. The New Covenant in Christ's blood fulfilled the requirements of the Old Covenant for redemption. The blood of Christ is seen as surpassing the blood sacrifices of the Old Covenant and eternally satisfying the requirements of a holy God.

Read: Colossians 1:13–14; John 14:6

Questions:

Do you ever attempt to approach God on the basis of "religious works" or performance? How?

✎ _____

_____

_____

_____

In what way does the blood of Jesus mean freedom and liberation for you?

_____

_____

_____

Kingdom Life—*Attain a Right Relationship with God*

The goal of the blood covenant is to bring us into a full and complete relationship with God as our Father; to restore us to the unity and "at-one-ment" we were meant to enjoy with Him.

Take some time now to read 2 Samuel 11 and 12 and Psalm 51. In these passages, we find the story of David's sin in regard to Bathsheba and his transparency before the Lord following his conviction for and repentance of his sin. This is an example of why King David was called "a man after God's own heart" (1 Samuel 13:14).

The key here is that David confessed his sin and did not attempt to cover it up with "religious works." He did not repeat the mistake of Adam and Eve who, when found out by God, attempted to hide, or Cain who brought his own offering to God. David took full advantage of the blood of the covenant. He did not seek to be justified by his "works." Rather, David offered to God the sacrifice of a "broken and contrite heart."

Read: Matthew 15:8–9; Romans 3:20–28

Questions:

How are transparency and honesty before God keys to spiritual vitality?

_____

_____

_____

On what basis can we be confident when we come before God asking to be cleansed spiritually?

✎ _____

_____

_____

In what way(s) have you depended on works rather than on the sufficiency of Christ's sacrifice?

✎ _____

_____

_____

_____

Kingdom Life—*Honest Before God*

The great sin of humankind is that we seek to justify ourselves through our own good works. Sometimes we even put on an outward show of spirituality. Yet God delights in people whose hearts are completely open before Him, hearts that are sensitive to His calling. When we come before God in praise and worship and allow the glory of His presence to create in us a tenderness and openness, then God can create a clean heart in us through His blood. The result of this openness before God is that He restores to us the joy of our salvation, without which we cannot evangelize the lost and reclaim our culture for Christ. Without restoration of the joy of salvation, we become dry bones and whitewashed tombs, as had the Pharisees (Matthew 23:27).

The blood of Jesus Christ makes it possible for us to come to God just as we are. We find cleansing and deliverance from the bondages of sin. We can receive a fresh infilling of His Spirit and have the joy of our salvation restored through the blood of the Lamb. Once we have been washed clean in His blood, we begin to walk in awesome spiritual beauty and His glory radiates through us. The result is that people are won to Jesus Christ, and the power of the Adversary is destroyed.

Kingdom Extra

The Old Testament (Old Covenant) pointed the way to the blood of Jesus Christ in the New Covenant. The writer of Hebrews 9:11–14 wrote that Jesus Christ, through His own blood, entered the Most Holy Place once and for all to obtain eternal redemption. The Mosaic covenant provided animal sacrifices with an earthly altar, which was symbolic of God's eternal and heavenly altar. The New Covenant is the eternal fulfillment of God's covenant, because it destroyed the power of sin and death forever. It is freely available to anyone who will accept it.

In Ephesians 1:7 we read, "In Him we have *redemption through His blood*, the forgiveness of sins, according to the riches of His grace." The blood of the covenant culminated in redemption through Jesus Christ.

Word Wealth

Redemption, *apolutrosis* (ap-ol-oo'-tro-sis); Strong's #629: A release secured by the payment of a ransom, deliverance, setting free. The word in secular Greek described a conqueror releasing prisoners, a master ransoming a slave, and redemption from an alien yoke. In the New Testament it designates deliverance through Christ from evil and the penalty of sin. The price paid to purchase that liberation was His shed blood.

Kingdom Life—*Ransomed and Redeemed*

Redemption involves the paying of ransom; but to whom is the ransom paid? Dr. Jack Hayford answers this question in his Citywide Bible Study. He notes that the price was the blood of Jesus and outlines four possible points of payment: "(a) Satan; (b) impersonal force of evil or death; (c) God and/or (d) the created order of things."

Dr. Hayford comments that Satan had no legal right to claim payment. Death and evil, though real, are abstract forces that cannot require payment. Thus, it was God's justice that *did* need to be satisfied, "but not," he observes, "in the sense that God was demanding payment as any human offended party might."

The need for justice was not offence against God as much as the fact that the order of things fundamental to God's nature had been violated. God's nature existed long before man's creation, sin, or fall. The universe was created with and through holiness. It is this holiness and this justice that must be answered to. In Jack Hayford's words, "Only the blood of Jesus could provide that answer."

Christianity is not just an archaic belief system in which men invented a blood-stained deity similar to the gods of pagan cultures, whose worship required sacrifice. The death force of sin unleashed into the world through man's disobedience can only be removed by a cosmic process of redemption through the sacrificial blood of Jesus Christ. This is not because God is some kind of offended being who demands retribution, but because of the real "order of things." In other words, the universe is a complete system of holiness, love, and justice. Therefore, violation of the laws of the universe produces certain results. Those results can only be undone by the application of higher laws that find their complete expression in salvation by grace and the blood of Jesus Christ.

What this means, on the practical level, is that God designed the universe to work a certain way, just as an engineer would create an automobile engine to run on a particular fuel. When trying to get that car engine to run, it doesn't matter how sincere you are. If you try to put anything other than gasoline in that engine, it simply will not work. In much the same way, it is only through the blood of Jesus that our sins can be forgiven.

Read: Romans 3:26; Hebrews 9:22

Questions:

Why was the blood necessary in order for redemption to occur?

How have you experienced the power of redemption in your own life?

✎ _____

_____

Many in our culture view references to the blood of Jesus Christ as primitive and arising from ignorance. How does the blood of Jesus Christ answer the basic problems of individuals and society-at-large?

✎ _____

_____

_____

Record Your Thoughts

We understand from the Bible that God is a "covenant maker" and that He has revealed Himself to us through His Word and through His Son. We can come to Him through the blood of the covenant because it is only the blood that can cleanse us from sin. Ultimately, the blood of Jesus Christ means complete liberation—shedding the shackles of sin and being loosed from bondage to harmful lifestyles.

Consider how these facts impact the false belief that there are many ways to God and how you might answer those who argue against the truth: Jesus is the only way to the Father.

Finally, list the ways in which the blood of the covenant and the sacrifice of Jesus Christ make it possible for you to find true freedom in life. Keep this list close by and refer to it often as an encouragement as you learn to walk as a partaker of the New Covenant.

SESSION TWO

The Authority
of God's Word

2 Timothy 3:16–17 All Scripture is given by inspiration of God, and is profitable for doctrine, for reproof, for correction, for instruction in righteousness, that the man of God may be complete, thoroughly equipped for every good work.

The absolute authority of the Bible over our lives is based in our conviction that this Book does not merely *contain* the Word of God, but that it *is* the Word of God in its sum and in its parts. This text testifies to this, describing the actual process of this inspiration (inbreathing of life):

1. The Bible is the word of the Holy Spirit. *Theopneustos* (Greek), translated "inspiration of God," literally means "God-breathed." This describes the source of the whole Bible's derivation as transcendent of human inspiration. The Bible is not the product of elevated human consciousness or enlightened human intellect, but is directly "breathed" from God Himself.

2. 2 Peter 1:20–21 elaborates this truth and adds that none of what was given was merely the private opinion of the writer and that each writer involved in the production of the Holy Scriptures was "moved by" (literally, "being borne along") the Holy Spirit. This does not mean the writers were merely robots, seized upon by God's power to write automatically without their conscious participation. God does not override those gifts of intellect and sensitivity that He has given His creatures. Beware of all

instances where individuals claim to "automatically" write anything at any time, for the Holy Spirit never functions that way.

3. 1 Corinthians 2:10–13 expounds on this process by which the revelation of the Holy Scriptures was given. This passage tells us that even the words used in the giving of the Bible (not just the ideas, but the precise terminology) were planned by the Holy Spirit, who deployed the respective authors of the Bible books to write, "comparing spiritual things with spiritual" (literally, "matching spiritual words to spiritual ideas"). This biblical view of the Bible's derivation is called the plenary verbal inspiration of the Scriptures, meaning every word is inspired by the Holy Spirit of God.

Read Psalm 19:7–8; Matthew 5:17–19, 24:35; Luke 16:17; John 10:35.

Questions:

How do these verses impact your view of God's Word?

What reason do we have to believe that there are absolutes in life? (Luke 16:17)

Since all Scripture is "God-breathed," it is absolute in its authority over the lives of men. Have the beliefs and attitudes of society caused you to question the inerrancy of Scripture in any way? Why or why not?

Behind the Scenes

Today, as in years past, the truth that the Bible is divinely inspired is a key issue. On all fronts, the divine inspiration of the Bible is under attack, even within the evangelical community.

Many theologians are forced to defend the issue of the divine inspiration of the Bible as the watershed issue of the Christian world. Major denominations, once orthodox in their theology, have attempted to embrace cultural reason and whim in their theology. Such issues as whether or not to make the Bible gender neutral emerge. People attempt to make God neither male nor female. In fact, the concept of God the Father is often questioned, as well as issues of human sexuality.

In Luke 16:17, Jesus said, "And it is easier for heaven and earth to pass away than for one tittle of the law to fail." God's Word is not subject to politically correct thinking. The truth of the Word is eternal and does not change with the passing whims of a culture.

Kingdom Life—*Truth is Absolute*

In understanding the concept of the authority of the Bible, it is important to understand the following concepts:

Cultural relativism is a secular world view in which no absolute right or wrong exists in the universe. In other words, everything is relative. This belief system stems from the idea that there is no God and that man is the center of the universe. It is an expression of modern humanism wherein absolutely everything is up for questioning, including the authority of the Scripture.

Absolutes is a term conveying the idea there are fixed laws that are not subject to human opinion. In other words, there is a right and a wrong. God's Word is absolute. While humanists would declare there are no absolutes, those embracing a Judeo-Christian worldview believe that absolutes most certainly exist and are not subject to popular opinion of the moment.

Final reality describes the fact that reality exists in a certain form and is not subject to popular opinion. In other words, final reality is what is real and true. The fact that Jesus Christ rose from the dead is final reality. Whether or not people choose to accept this does not alter the reality that it happened. That is final reality.

Read Psalm 119:9–16.

Questions:

What does it mean to hide the Word of God in your heart?

_____

_____

_____

How can this protect us from sin?

_____

_____

_____

What further insight can you gain from this passage in regard to the importance of knowing the Word of God?

_____

_____

_____

Kingdom Life—*Hold on to the Rock*

The blood of Christ and the Word of God are two constants in the divine order of things. They are linked together and both are fundamental to the covenant of God. Here is the link:

The Word *reveals* the need for the blood.

The blood *seals* the covenant of the Word. Both are inviolable as absolute authority.

The Word, the absolute authority of heaven's throne.

The blood, the absolute authority vanquishing sin's power.

Edward Mote captured this idea in the third verse and chorus of his grand old hymn "The Solid Rock":

> His oath, His covenant, His blood
> Support me in the whelming flood;
> When all around my soul gives way
> He then is all my hope and stay.
>
> *Chorus:*
> On Christ the solid Rock I stand;
> All other ground is sinking sand.
> All other ground is sinking sand.

Probing the Depths

It is amazing to find the degree of dissimilarity and dispute that exists within the scientific community. In the field of psychology, for instance, there are many schools of thought. Though psychology is taught as a science, every major psychological theorist seems to contradict or disagree with his predecessors. The reason for this disparity in the understanding and practice of psychology is that the theories on which the science is based are subjective—based on the perceptions and opinions of men.

However, the Word of God is not subjective; it is not subject to change; it is God-breathed and the final authority in the lives of God's people. Those who choose to believe in the inerrancy and infallibility of God's Word are not religious legalists whose minds are shut to other opinions; they are not frightened by creative thinking or the exploration of philosophies. Those who believe that the Bible is the Word of God do so because of their conviction and whole-hearted belief that the entirety of the Bible is divinely inspired. They choose to believe the Bible above the opinions, philosophies, and writings of men, which constantly change.

Kingdom Life—*God's Word Guides our Lives*

Read Psalm 119:89–91.

God's Word is settled. It is final reality. In other words, it is true—not just in religious or spiritual matters. It is true in every area of life because God created all of life and the universe. He understands how it functions. We must get away from the notion that somehow God is intimidated by computers, technology, DNA molecules, sex, and so on. God is the Creator of humankind and the universe. He is light years beyond our present level of scientific and social development.

It is important to understand that Christianity is Truth and not a religion! God's Word is not just true because you and I choose to believe in it. It is true, because on an objective scientific basis it is simply true. When we understand this reality, it should give us confidence in our daily living and relating to our society.

Read 1 Peter 1:25; John 14:6.

Questions:

Why is it important to understand why God's Word is the final authority in life?

✎ _____

_____

Define the expression "Christianity is Truth and not a religion."

✎ _____

_____

What does the fact that "Christianity is Truth and not a religion" mean to your everyday life? How does it give you confidence to share your faith?

✎ _____

_____

Probing the Depths

Many Christians are intimidated by science and reason. Though they might not admit it consciously, they may question whether the Bible is really true when it comes to scientific, social, or historic matters. They wonder if the story of Adam and Eve, Noah and the ark, Moses' parting the Red Sea, and so on are just myths to guide us. These Christians do not have confidence and boldness in their faith. Their faith has been undermined, and they live on the defensive because they have never discovered for themselves the reality of the Bible's truthfulness in all areas of life.

Some Christians may fear sending their children to college; others may be afraid of intense study in fields such as biology, medicine, psychology, and physics for fear of losing their faith. The problem is that these people have a faith built on a religious experience that somehow has become separated from reason. They do not have the proper intellectual foundation for their faith. They have embraced cultural relativism which results in a weakened view of Scripture. They do not understand that Christianity is Truth and not a religion.

The importance of the Word of God as the final authority is addressed by the most influential theologians, evangelists, and ministers who met in 1974 at the Lausanne Conference. They issued this statement on the authority of God's Word: "We affirm the divine inspiration, truthfulness and authority of both Old and New Testament Scriptures in their entirety as the only written Word of God, without error in all that it affirms." [1]

This is a key issue in individual Christian lives as well as in society at large. As Christians, we cannot allow tolerance and accommodation to weaken our faith and our witness. We must hold to the incontrovertible truth that the Bible is true in all that it teaches, whether those teachings regard religious matters, morality, science, or human conduct. It is imperative that we, as children of God, integrate the truth of God's Word and the authority of Scripture into our lives.

---

1. Stott, John. "LOP 3: The Lausanne Covenant: An Exposition and Commentary." *The Lausanne Movement.* Lausanne Commiteee for World Evangelization, 1975. Web. 08 Apr. 2011.

Read Psalm 19:7–11, 119:9–11; John 1:1–2; 1 Corinthians 6:19–20.

Questions:

How does the authority of God's Word affect your life in matters of morality?

_____

_____

_____

How does the authority of God's Word affect your life in areas of sexuality?

_____

_____

_____

How does the authority of God's Word affect your understanding of creation in relationship to the theory of evolution?

_____

_____

_____

_____

Probing the Depths

The reliability and authority of God's Word are directly tied into the fact that God and His Word are one. In John 1:1–5, 14, the apostle John states that God and His Word are one and the same. Genesis 1:26 says, "Let Us make man in Our image, according to Our likeness." Here God refers to Himself as plural, which makes reference to the Deity as a Triune Being—God the Father, God the Son, and God the Spirit. That is why it is possible for the Scripture to say, "In the beginning was the Word, and the Word was with God, and the Word was God."

This makes the Bible unique among all other spiritual books because here God claims to be one with His Word. In fact, "God and His Word are one" also disproves the truthfulness and reliability of other so-called spiritual books, such as the *Book of Mormon*, the Hindu *Upanishads* or the *Bhagavad Gita*, and the *Koran* of the Muslim religion. These books claim to be enlightened or to include special revelations. Clearly, if God and His Word are one, then He cannot contradict Himself. Therefore, these other books, which claim to be words of God, must be false because they contain things which contradict the Bible. They cannot be simultaneously true. The final proof of the authority of God's Word is the fact that Jesus Christ, who is the Word, resurrected from the dead. No other religious teacher in history has conquered death. It is the resurrection of Jesus Christ, who is the Word of God, which proves once and for all the ultimate power, authority, and credence of the Bible.

Read John 18:37; James 1:22.

Questions:

What does the fact that "God and His Word are one" say about the truthfulness of the Word of God?

_____

_____

_____

Why is it impossible for other so-called spiritual books to be true?

_____

_____

_____

If God and His Word are one, then what should your personal response be to anything you read in the Bible?

_____

_____

_____

Behind the Scenes

Today, many people have serious questions regarding doctrines, teachings, and beliefs. In all of these matters of doctrine and teaching, it is the Scripture which is to be the final authority. There is a need to not only judge everything in the light of the Scripture, but also to recognize that the body of Christ is one body. Great care must be exercised to make sure that we uphold the authority of Scripture. We cannot compromise key doctrines, such as the virgin birth of Jesus Christ and the fact of His resurrection. However, there are other beliefs that are not pivotal issues. Unity should never be built through a weakened view of Scripture.

Yet, under the lordship of Jesus Christ and the authority of His Word, there is room for diverse styles of worship and emphasis. It is here we must allow the love of God to fill us that we may love all members of the body of Christ, even though they may fellowship with different denominations. Without compromising Scripture, we must avoid a non-biblical smallness of heart and allow the Holy Spirit to develop in us an unselfish and passionate love for one another. Jesus said, "A new commandment I give to you, that you love one another; as I have loved you, that you also love one another. By this all will know that you are My disciples, if you have love for one another" (John 13:34, 35).

Record Your Thoughts

Write down some subjects of doctrine about which you have questions or over which you may have heard arguments.

What scriptural evidence do you have to support or reject each one?

In what way(s) can knowing Scripture aid you in realizing the infallibility of God's Word?

What steps can you take to become more knowledgeable about God's Word?

SESSION THREE

Obey the Word of God

 Kingdom Key—*Guard Your Heart*

Psalm 119:11 Your word I have hidden in my heart, that I might not sin against You!

In Psalm 119:89, we read, "Forever, O Lord, Your word is settled in heaven." This text asserts the all-encompassing, absolutely authoritative Word of God as unchangingly secured in heaven. God's rule by His Word is timeless. Though times and seasons change, though social customs, human opinions, and philosophical viewpoints vary, they have no effect on the constancy or authority of God's Word.

God is faithful in applying the power, promise, and blessing of His Word, along with its requirements of justice and judgment. Just as He spoke and the Earth was created and is sustained, so He has spoken regarding His laws for living. The relativism of human thought does not affect His authority or standards.

While creation abides by His Word, man is often a study in contrast to this submission to the Creator's authority. However, whatever our past rebellion, upon coming to Christ, a practical reinstatement of God's Word as the governing principle for all our life is to take place. As spiritual people, we are to refuse the natural inclinations of fallen men. As we hear and yield to the authority of God's Word, we verify that we are no longer dominated by the world's spirit error.

Read Proverbs 4:20–23.

Questions:

Is Scripture the guiding authority of your life? How can this be seen by others?

✎ _____

_____

_____

Do you spend sufficient time reading, studying, and meditating on God's Word? What affect do you believe this has on your ability to walk in obedience to God's will for your life?

✎ _____

_____

_____

 Kingdom Life—*Know the Consequence of Disobedience*

To prepare for this section and ones to follow, read chapters 2 and 3 of Genesis.

In the very beginning of time, God created Paradise for Adam and Eve to live in and enjoy. It was a perfect world, answering the deepest needs of humanity. Adam and Eve lived in perfect peace in this magnificent paradise.

The only commandment God gave Adam and Eve, He gave for their own good. God knew that if Adam and Eve ate of the tree of the knowledge of good and evil, a death force called "sin" would enter the human race, destroying them and their world. Far from being unreasonable, God was trying to protect Adam and Eve from certain destruction. God gave His Word to Adam and Eve in the form of a commandment to protect them and give them life. The result of Adam and Eve's choice to disobey the Word of God was death and destruction. This same principle holds true today. God gives His Word to humankind in the form of commandments for the purpose of protecting and giving life.

Deep within the psyche of modern man is an innate drive to return to Paradise. Subconsciously, modern man knows that he was created for a better world. Traffic jams, pollution, violence, war, disease, strife, poverty, shortages, and unpaid bills are not normal. They are outgrowths of the Fall of Man, which began when Adam and Eve were banished from Paradise.

Read Psalm 12:6–7; Proverbs 30:5

Questions:

In what way(s) have you experienced God's Word being "tried in a furnace"?

✎ _____

_____

_____

In practical application, how can God's Word daily protect and add to your life?

✎ _____

_____

_____

How can knowing the Word of God allow you to figuratively return to "paradise"?

✎ _____

_____

_____

Probing the Depths

Read the fourth chapter of Luke. Here, Jesus confronts Satan and dramatically exposes the adversary's relationship to this present world. Note the significance in Satan's offer to Jesus of "all the kingdoms of the world." Here we see the adversary as administrator of the curse on this planet, a role he has held since man's dominion was lost and forfeited at the Fall. Because of this, Jesus does not contest the Devil's right to offer him the world's kingdoms and glory, but He pointedly denies the terms offered by Satan. Jesus knows He is here to regain and ultimately win them, but He will do so on the Father's terms, not the Adversary's. Still, the present world systems are largely grounded by the limited but powerful and destructive rule of the one Jesus calls "the ruler of this world" (John 12:31). Understanding these facts, we are wise not to attribute to God anything of the disorder of our confused, sin-riddled, diseased, tragedy-ridden, and tormented planet. "This present evil age" (Galatians 1:4) "lies under the sway of the wicked one" (1 John 5:19). But Jesus also said that Satan's rule "will be cast down," and that he "has nothing in Me," that is, no control over Christ or Christ's own. "He who is in you is greater than he who is in the world" (1 John 4:4).

Kingdom Life—*Trust God's Goodness*

The purpose of God's giving us His Word in the form of a commandment is to bring us abundant life and to protect us. It is never God's intention to restrict us: the Word of God is always a protector and liberator.

At times, God's commandments seem difficult or harsh, especially when we want to go our own way. The commandments are always designed to produce the maximum fulfillment in our life. The root issue, in relationship to God's Word, is trusting God's goodness. When we understand the fact that God is our loving Heavenly Father and always wants the best for us, then we can have total confidence that His Word and His commandments are always for our best interests.

Read John 14:23–24; 1 John 2:3–6, 3:22–24, 5:2–5.

Questions:

How are obedience to the Word of God and our love for our Lord linked?

What are the primary results of a life lived in obedience to the Word of God?

✎ _____

_____

_____

How might the realization of the unbreakable connection between obedience *to* God and love *for* God impact your life in the future?

✎ _____

_____

_____

Kingdom Life—*Overcome the Enemy*

In Genesis 3:1–7, we are introduced to several key components regarding disobedience to the Word of God, the Fall of Man, and the reality of the Devil—the "serpent of old" (Revelation 12:9). At this turning point of human history, we learn several important facts about human nature, the reality of evil, and the results of disobeying God's Word.

First, we discover that there is a real, evil force in the universe that had a specific agenda in tempting Adam and Eve to sin. Satan maneuvered for the ultimate power play—the dominion of humankind—a tactic that proved successful when Adam and Eve disobeyed God's Word.

But God has enabled His people to walk free of Satan's otherwise successful scheme. In Revelation 12:11 we are told, "And they overcame him [Satan] by the blood of the Lamb and by the word of their testimony." In other words, it is through our faith and obedience to the Word of God that we gain the power to overcome Satan (1 John 5:5). It is a very simple concept: obedience to the Word of God enables us to overcome Satan; disobedience to the Word of God enables Satan to overcome us.

We also discover in the exchange between Satan and Eve that Satan twists and lies about God's Word. The Apostle John referred to Satan as the "father of lies." Our enemy will continue as he began, he will always seek to cause us to deny, disbelieve, or distort the Word of God.

Read Revelation 12:11; 2 Corinthians 11:3; James 4:4–10.

Questions:

In what area(s) of your life do you find you are most easily deceived by Satan's attempt to misrepresent God's Word?

✎_____

_____

_____

_____

How can knowing God's Word enable you to more effectively resist Satan's attempts to overcome you?

✎_____

_____

_____

_____

What steps can you take today to begin holding more closely to God's Word?

✎_____

_____

_____

_____

Behind the Scenes

Immediately after Adam and Eve ate of the forbidden fruit, their spiritual natures were short-circuited. Eating of the tree of the knowledge of good and evil produced a total change in their consciousness. Adam and Eve, who had walked in complete peace and joy in the presence of God, now felt an intense separation from Him. For the first time, fear entered their minds and hearts. Their innocence was lost and they knew they were naked, not just physically but spiritually. Their immediate response was to attempt to cover their nakedness through their own effort, so they sewed "fig leaves together and made themselves coverings" (Genesis 3:7).

When Adam and Eve heard the sound of the Lord God walking, their hearts no longer rejoiced; instead, they felt both fear and shame. Their supernatural relationship with God had become polluted and fearful, so they attempted to hide their nakedness with "fig leaves." But this effort toward self-covering was ridiculous because they were not just naked physically but spiritually. When God asked them, "Who told you that you were naked?" He did not have to be told they had eaten of the tree of the knowledge of good and evil. The very atmosphere of the Garden of Eden had changed. God instantly knew when they had eaten of the fruit because He could sense the separation of Adam and Eve from His intimate presence and He understood the devastating destruction that sin would bring about.

 ### Kingdom Life—*Return to Intimacy*

In Genesis 3:21 we read, "Also for Adam and his wife the Lord God made tunics of skin, and clothed them." Here we see that God provided a covering for them through the sacrifice of innocent animals. The sacrifice of innocent animals was a foreshadowing of the blood of the covenant. God was covering the nakedness and sin of Adam and Eve through a substitutionary sacrifice. Only God could undo the power of sin, as He would later do through the blood of Jesus Christ.

Adam and Eve's disobedience to the word of God allowed Satan to gain dominion over humankind and caused death and destruction to enter the human race. However, God began a plan to restore humankind's dominion over the planet through the blood of the covenant.

Read Romans 5:14–21.

Questions:

Jesus can be called the second Adam. Why is this so?

✎ _____

_____

_____

_____

What is your understanding of "dominion"?

✎ _____

_____

_____

_____

How might you use what you have learned thus far in this study to begin walking in the dominion Christ has re-established for those who belong to Him?

✎ _____

_____

_____

_____

Record Your Thoughts

We live in a society wherein the commandments of God are often totally ignored. Consider the controversies and laws regarding abortion and marriage. In what other ways do you see that society has fallen for the lying, deceitful, and manipulative schemes of the enemy?

Think of areas in your own life in which you have disobeyed God, and write down the ways you have actually lost control and power due to disobedience. Consider how God's grace has intervened in these areas.

SESSION FOUR

Justified by Faith

 Kingdom Key—*Find Victory through Faith*

Romans 5:1–2 Therefore, having been justified by faith, we have peace with God through our Lord Jesus Christ, through whom also we have access by faith into this grace in which we stand, and rejoice in hope of the glory of God.

The truth in these verses brings believers to a place of genuine freedom where we are free to obey God, not to obtain His favor, but because He has already given us His favor. Within His unconditional acceptance given to us because of what Christ has done, we are freed from the need to monitor our behavior and loosed into the joy of knowing His friendship. Focusing primarily on our attempts at righteousness only diverts our attention from His loveliness, which ultimately erodes our dependence on Him to produce in us the beauty of His character. Grace underscores the generosity of God's love, highlighting the truth that God does not coerce change by threatening us. Instead, He conquers by lavishing His love upon us. His grace frees us from wearying, self-generated endeavors and releases us to allow His Holy Spirit within "to will and to do for His good pleasure" (Philippians 2:13).

Read Genesis 4:1–10.

Questions:

Cain attempted to approach God on his own terms and with his own ideas. How is this way of thinking reflected in the humanistic philosophies and man-made religions of today?

Cain approached God on the basis of his own works and self-effort and, in effect, violated the blood covenant by refusing to bring to God the sacrifice He demanded. In what ways do you find yourself offering works to God rather than the sacrifice He requires?

✎ _____

_____

_____

Probing the Depths

Cain approached God on the basis of his own works and self-effort. In distinct contrast, Abel approached God through the blood of the covenant. Earlier in Genesis 3:21, we read how God made tunics of animal skin for Adam and Eve in the first blood covering. God had already established the blood of the covenant. It stated that after the Fall, man could only come to God through a blood sacrifice. In addition, God had already rejected the self-made covering of fig leaves by Adam and Eve. Since this information had been passed on to Cain and Abel, Cain had no excuse in violating the blood covenant.

The story of Cain and Abel represents the two different philosophical streams of humankind—1) those who obey the Word of God and approach God through the blood covenant (Abel) and 2) those who disobey the Word of God and attempt to come to God on their own terms or ideas (Cain).

The living God of the universe went to great lengths to communicate with humankind the need for a blood covenant. This communication has bridged centuries of civilization and has been confirmed with powerful miracles that found their full expression in the death and resurrection of Jesus Christ in real space-time history. Therefore, men and women are really without any excuse when they choose to reject God's chosen method of salvation by faith in Jesus Christ through the blood covenant.

Modern humanism, with all its emphasis on humanly energized and resourced programs of self-esteem and self-actualization, is really the religion of Cain who offered the fruit of his own work to

God. Of course, there is nothing wrong with self-esteem or purpose-ful pursuit of life's goals when they flow from a right relationship with God. It is interesting to note that, in response to God's rejection of his offering, Cain became very angry and murdered his brother, Abel. Ultimately, those who have come to God with the fruit of their own offering become angry and begin to persecute those who have come to God through the blood. This is why, throughout history, both Christians and Jews have been persecuted. It also explains why, in our time, some who have embraced humanism have embarked on a campaign to eradicate Christianity from our culture. It is the hatred of Cain expressed in contemporary terms. Men and women will either surrender to the lordship of Jesus Christ through the blood covenant or they will be ruled by the powers of darkness because of their rejec-tion of God's way.

It is important that we understand the spiritual root of all false religions, including the religion of humanism. Despite its false pre-tenses at being a science, humanism is nothing more than a false reli-gion with its own doctrines and its own patron saints. It requires faith that is separated from reason by its followers as well as the same kind of blind allegiance that any other cult would demand.

Kingdom Life—*Find Salvation through the Cross*

When Cain deliberately rejected God's provision through the blood cov-ering and came to God on his own terms, he became the spiritual father of all those who, throughout history, have rejected God's plan of salvation. Hinduism, Buddhism, the teachings of Muhammad, and all the religious cults that stem from these teachings set forth a program of salvation through self-effort and religious works. Humanism espouses that there is no God and man must save himself. All these blasphemous schools of thought reflect the sin of Cain—they reject God's truth in favor of a man-made religion wherein man becomes the center of the universe.

In our time, humanism has has found expression in the mysticism of the New Age Movement. This and other ungodly, age-old, religious cults are renewing their influence upon our day. By money and media, pagan religious views are spreading around the world and popularizing human philosophies of salvation without Christ or the Cross.

The statements above are not born of hateful attitudes toward other religions. Rather they are concerns over 1) the insufficiency of systems sincerely seeking God but tragically missing Him, and 2) the need to know the difference so that we may both steadfastly and sensitively reach out to the lost of our generation.

Read John 14:6; Ephesians 2.

Questions:

Does your life reflect the truth of salvation through Christ and not your own efforts?

_____

_____

What other Scripture passages can you locate that clearly teach salvation is found only in the sacrifice of our Lord and His resurrection from the dead?

_____

_____

 Kingdom Life—*Find True Righteousness*

In sharp contrast to all those who attempt to come to God on their own terms, there are those who seek to come to God on His terms—through the blood of the covenant. They mirror the obedience to God exemplified by Abel. He obeyed God and came to Him through a blood covenant in which he offered God the firstborn of his flock. Throughout the Bible, we find that men and women are justified before God through their faith in God's promise and not through their own works.

It is important that we understand how God's law of putting men into right relationship with Himself actually works. Nowhere does the Bible teach that by performing religious duties men and women can earn their righteousness! This makes the teaching of Christianity completely unique among every other religion in the world. Islam teaches that its believers must adhere to a strict set of commandments and religious practices. Many cults teach their followers that they must complete many religious programs in order to earn their righteousness before God. The New Age Movement, based on ancient Hinduism and Buddhism, teaches that we must work off our *karma* (the quality of this life and future lives based upon behavior in current and past lives).

However, the Bible teaches something completely different.

Read Romans 4:2–3; Ephesians 2:8.

Questions:

What is your understanding of the word "righteous"?

_____

_____

A sinful heart attitude is reflected in one who attempts to gain a right standing before God through works. What is that sinful attitude?

_____

_____

_____

Do you see areas of your own life where this attitude prevails?

_____

_____

_____

What steps can you take to cleanse your life of a self-sufficient spirit?

_____

_____

_____

Word Wealth—*Accounted*

Accounted, *logidzomai* (log-id'-zom'ahee); Strong's #3049: Compare "logistic" and "logarithm." Numerically, to count, compute, calculate, sum up. Metaphorically, to consider, reckon, reason, deem, evaluate, value. *Logidzomai* finalizes thought, judges matters, draws logical conclusions, decides outcomes, and puts every action into a debit or credit position (Romans 4:3).

Kingdom Life—*Enjoy Right Standing Before God*

King David was called "a man after God's own heart." Yet he committed murder and adultery. David paid a heavy price for those sins in his life. However, through the blood and his faith in God's ability to make him righteous, he was made righteous before God. God hates sin. We will reap the consequences of the sins we commit, in terms of the emotional, psychological, and physical debris that sin brings. However, if we repent and choose to accept God's gift of righteousness in Jesus Christ, we can enjoy right standing with God.

We must realize, however, that there is nothing we can do to earn this right standing. *All* of our attempts to make ourselves holy and pure before God are useless. God is not interested in our religious duties and good works as a means of approaching Him. God does want us to love people and do good things. However, things we do, in terms of ministry and good works, do not earn us points with God. If we are reading the Bible, tithing, praying, and doing good works because we are trying to move up some invisible scale of spirituality, then we are missing the point. All those actions are important for our spiritual growth, and they benefit us. But they do not earn God's approval! God already totally approves of us because of our faith in what Jesus Christ has done.

Read Isaiah 64:6; Romans 10:3–4; Hebrews 11:6; 1 John 1:9.

Questions:

What is your current understanding of righteousness through faith?

_____

_____

_____

What areas of your life have not been submitted to and cleansed by Christ?

_____

_____

_____

How might surrendering these areas of bondage allow you to experience the freedom and dominion that are meant to be yours?

_____

_____

_____

Kingdom Extra

It is vitally important that we understand the powerful, biblical truth that "the just shall live by faith." When ministering to people about the gospel, we should always remember that God will meet them exactly where they are and they *never* have to clean themselves up first. In actuality, an individual cannot be cleansed through their own efforts; the Holy Spirit works inside a person, bringing a total cleansing from the inside out.

It is Jesus Christ who, through the power of the Spirit within us, purifies and gives us the power to become victorious. Christianity is not a matter of trying to be holy and doing good works. Christianity is about a personal relationship with Jesus Christ. We become holy and minister good works not as a means of trying to become righteous, but rather, as the power of Jesus Christ fills us, we naturally become more like Him.

Record Your Thoughts

Having dealt with the theme of righteousness by faith alone, how would you apply this truth to your own life?

How would you apply what you have studied to your personal relationship with people you work with or live around who don't know Christ?

How would this truth affect your approach in witnessing to them?

Briefly, write your current understanding of what it means to be People of the Covenant. Later in this study, you will be asked again to state your understanding of this important identity. Refer back to this section at that time and compare your answers. You may be amazed at how much your understanding has grown.

SESSION FIVE

The Blood of Jesus

 Kingdom Key—*A New and Living Way*

Hebrews 10:19–22 Therefore, brethren, having boldness to enter the Holiest by the blood of Jesus, by a new and living way which He consecrated for us, through the veil, that is, His flesh, and having a High Priest over the house of God, let us draw near with a true heart in full assurance of faith, having our hearts sprinkled from an evil conscience and our bodies washed with pure water.

Jesus came to make a way where there was no way—no approach to Father God in a loving and worshipful relationship, and no path to meaningful and victorious living. He is our High Priest—the High Priest of a New Covenant sealed by His blood.

We learn in the Old Testament that God instituted what is called the Mosaic Covenant, with animal sacrifices provided to offer temporary covering for man's sin and guilt. These animal sacrifices constituted the first blood covenant of the Old Testament—the Old Covenant. These animal sacrifices were conducted annually at a tabernacle that was symbolic of God's eternal altar.

In the Levitical sacrifices, the worshipers were not made perfect. Animal sacrifices had to be repeated yearly. The ancient tabernacle had to be sanctified by the blood of these animals. The Old Testament sacrifices were merely earthly copies of the heavenly altar.

What both the Old Testament and the New Testament teach us is that God is a totally holy Being whose very presence cannot tolerate sin. The holy presence of God literally destroys sin with a burning, purifying fire. Obviously, since man has been contaminated by sin, he would be destroyed instantly in the presence of God. Through the blood of Jesus Christ, God solved this problem. The blood of Jesus Christ actually takes away the sin from human beings so that God's presence can visit them without destroying them. It makes it possible for us to enter into the throne room of God, because it totally purifies us and redeems us from sin.

Read Hebrews 8 and 9.

Questions:

How is the New Covenant different from the Old Covenant?

✎ _____

_____

_____

_____

What is your current understanding of the "new and living way" Jesus has made available to you?

✎ _____

_____

_____

_____

_____

Word Wealth

Mercy seat, *hilasterion* (hil-as-tay'-ree-on); Strong's #2435: Although used only here and in Romans 3:25 in the New Testament, the word is quite common in the Septuagint (a Greek translation of the Hebrew Scriptures dating to the third and second centuries BC), where it primarily denotes the lid of gold above the Ark of the Covenant. Hebrews 9:5 reflects this meaning, indicating the place of atonement. The root meaning of *hilasterion* is that of appeasing and placating an offended god. Applied to the sacrifice of Christ, the word suggests that Christ's death was propitiatory (preparing the way for us to be reconciled to God), averting the wrath of God from the sinner.

Probing the Depths

Hebrews 10:19–22 declares the stark contrast between the message of Jesus Christ and every other religion. The millions of people who flock to Mecca, the hundreds of thousands who bathe in the holy river in India, the spiritual pilgrims who climb the heights of the Himalayan mountains in search of answers, the zealous Scientologists who spend hundreds of thousands of dollars to go up the "bridge" of enlightenment to experience being "clear" do not understand the liberating truth: because of the blood of Jesus Christ we now have direct access to God. We can enter into the very presence of God boldly with full assurance because of the blood of Jesus Christ.

Although at face value this truth may seem simple, it is that simplicity that makes the message of the gospel radically different from any of the religious systems on the face of the earth. The majority of religions and spiritual systems recognize that man is separated from God, but they have no real means of dealing with the problem. The blood of Jesus Christ actually deals with the sin problem by removing it from our lives.

Kingdom Life—*Receive a New Nature*

In Hebrews 8:7–13 we see the power of the New Covenant at work. The first covenant was an external covenant that set a standard by the Law; yet the power to live within the bounds of this covenant was not provided. Jesus' ministry is performed under the covenant of God's grace, wrought within the mind and hearts of believers by the power of the Holy Spirit. Thus, God established a new personal covenant relationship with His people, based not on a compelling force from without, but on an impelling power from within. The blood of Jesus Christ made it possible for us to be cleansed of our sins and enjoy intimate fellowship with God.

Our minds and hearts are renewed and our spiritual natures are regenerated by the blood of the Lamb. This is the "new and living way" referred to in Hebrews 10:20. The sin force set in action when Adam and

Eve disobeyed God is now undone. Through the blood of Jesus Christ and receiving forgiveness for our sins by accepting Jesus Christ into our lives and becoming "born-again," we receive a new nature. The Fall of Man is reversed in our hearts, and the powers of sin and death are broken; God has provided a way for each of us to return to Him. That way is through the blood of Jesus Christ. In John 14:6 Jesus Christ said, "I am the way, the truth, and the life. No one comes to the Father except through Me."

Jesus Christ is the way to God—the new and living way! The blood of Jesus Christ restores the relationship our ancestors, Adam and Eve, had with Him in the Garden of Eden.

Read Psalm 146; Philippians 3:8–11.

Questions:

How does this new and living way make it possible for you to experience victory in your life?

_____

_____

_____

Why is the reality that Jesus Christ is the "new and living way" cause for celebration?

_____

_____

_____

In what ways does your life reflect or fail to show forth the joy and peace of knowing and being reconnected to Father God?

_____

_____

_____

_____

Kingdom Life—Be Fully Alive

It would be a great tragedy to simply discuss the reality that Jesus Christ is the new and living way in merely spiritual terms. The profound reality is that Jesus' atoning work can have a revolutionary impact upon every aspect of our lives.

While modern psychotherapy, behavioral scientists, mood altering drugs, and the like can be helpful, they cannot change human nature. We cannot find true freedom in the coping strategies developed by man. Only the blood of Jesus Christ truly has the power to set free. The blood of Jesus Christ speaks powerfully to the multitude of relational and internal maladies we face.

We need to understand that all of our problems today stem from what happened in the Garden of Eden millennia ago. When man's spiritual nature died and spiritual darkness invaded the human consciousness and spirit, all the myriad problems within the human personality (for example, fear, anxiety, guilt, anger, bitterness, and all resultant psychological and relational disorders that stem from them) began to flow out of man's sinful nature.

It must be understood that, before the Fall, Adam and Eve did not have any of these problems—they were fully alive, spiritually, physically, and emotionally. God's presence filled and saturated their beings. Once that Holy presence of God was removed by the death force of sin, those problems became manifest.

The new and living way, made possible by the blood of Jesus Christ, restores us and allows us to experience full, abundant life—the life Adam and Eve once knew. Physical and mental healing, at every dimension, is made possible by the release of God's presence and glory. In a nutshell, behavioral therapy, biofeedback, mood altering drugs, and other techniques, while often helpful and sometimes necessary, fail to supply true freedom; the complete eradication of all vestiges of sin's destruction is only available through the blood of Jesus Christ. When God's glory and presence are released through the new and living way, which is the blood of Jesus, man is spiritually resurrected and restored to right relationship with God.

Read Ephesians 4:17–24.

Questions:

The "new and living way" made possible by the blood of Jesus is available to us. What must we do to access that "new and living way"?

✎ _____

_____

Based on what you have just read, why do you believe so many Christians suffer from the maladies (physical, spiritual, and emotional) that resulted from the fall of man?

✎ _____

_____

_____

According to Ephesians 4:17–24, what steps can and should be taken by those who so suffer?

✎ _____

_____

_____

 ## Kingdom Life—*Experience the Glory of God*

Read 2 Chronicles 7:1–3.

If the Old Testament animal sacrifices could release the glory of God so powerfully that the priests could not enter the temple because the glory of the Lord filled the house, think of how much more powerfully the glory and presence of God is released in the temples of our human personalities through the "new and living way," the blood of Jesus Christ. God wants His glory to fill the house of our personalities in an overflowing measure.

Jesus said, "Your heavenly Father [will] give the Holy Spirit to those who ask Him!" (Luke 11:13). In John 20:22 we read, "He breathed on them and said to them, 'Receive the Holy Spirit.' " (See also Acts 1:8.) Through Jesus Christ—the new and living way—the promise of the Holy Spirit is released. When we understand the provision that God made for us in the new and living way, through the blood of Jesus Christ and the indwelling of the Holy Spirit, we can open ourselves to this divine resource, and the glory of the Lord will fill our house—our very selves, the temple of the Holy Spirit of God.

Once again mankind can be filled and saturated with the holy presence and glory of God; the intimate presence and fellowship Adam and Eve knew with God in Eden can be restored. When the Holy Spirit of God is released upon men and women in a baptism of His healing glory, the problems manifested by man's sin nature begin to diminish and will progressively be overcome as faith's pathway of victory is learned.

The presence of God within us through the Holy Spirit puts God's laws in our hearts and minds because we become regenerated through the Word of God and the Holy Spirit, who is made available to us through the blood of the Lamb. The new and living way is both powerful and profound, releasing within the temples of our human personalities the same glory that filled the Old Testament temple—the *Shekinah* glory of God.

Read Romans 5:1–2; 1 Corinthians 3:16; 6:19–20.

Questions:

Why does God want His glory to fill the "house" of your personality in overflowing measure?

✎ _____

_____

_____

How can being filled regularly with the presence and glory of God affect your everyday life?

✎ _____

_____

_____

How does the provision that God made for us through the blood of Jesus Christ make it possible for us to experience God's glory at work in our lives?

✎ _____

_____

_____

_____

Word Wealth

Shekinah, (sha-kigh'-nuh): This is a Greek word meaning dwelling. *Shekinah* is not found within the pages of Scripture, but is frequently found in later Jewish writing. It is God's physical presence, which appears as a bright, luminous cloud (as God revealed His presence in the Tabernacle in the wilderness and in the Holy of Holies of Solomon's temple) or in the form of fire as when God spoke to Moses from the burning bush.

Record Your Thoughts

Apply the great truth found in Hebrews 10:19, 20. Go boldly to God through the new and living way, which is the blood of Jesus. Spend some time in prayer with God and draw near to Him in full assurance of faith. Begin by praising and worshiping Him. Ask Him to fill you with the glory of His presence. Ask Him to fill you afresh with His Holy Spirit.

List the areas of your life in which you struggle with bondage or any area in which you don't experience the abundant, full life God wants for you. Take each of these to God, asking for His touch. Ask Him to help you see where you may have failed to appropriate the new and living way available to you through Christ.

Allow the presence of God to overflow your personality; then praise Him for filling the empty places or problems of your life with divine glory. Rejoice in His magnificent presence and spend some time worshiping Him. Allow Him to bathe you in His light and glory and let any oppression in your life be completely lifted. Go ahead! Praise Him!

SESSION SIX

The Power
of God's Word

 Kingdom Key—*Rely Completely on the Word of God*

Hebrews 4:12 For the word of God is living and powerful, and sharper than any two-edged sword, piercing even to the division of soul and spirit, and of joints and marrow, and is a discerner of the thoughts and intents of the heart.

The Word of God contains the power to transform our world, not only externally, but internally. It moves into the depths of our being when we hear or read it. The word translated as "powerful" in Hebrews 4:12 is the Greek word *energes* (Strong's #1756), which is comparable in meaning to the English word "energetic." It denotes something at work, active, and effective.

When we read, study, meditate, or hear God's Word, we are receiving living energy into our beings and experiencing the very presence of God Himself. The result is regeneration and transformation—God's Word produces life.

The foundational constant in life is the authority and reliability of God's Word. People change, nations rise and fall, economies falter, and physical bodies decay. Yet, in the midst of earthly chaos, God's Word and the promises it contains are unshakable. God has given us a powerful and practical resource in His Word "that the man of God may be complete, thoroughly equipped for every good work" (2 Timothy 3:17).

Read Psalm 138:2; Matthew 4:4; John 1:1–2, 14:6; 1 Peter 2:2.

Questions:

How should the fact that God and His Word are one affect your reading and studying of the Bible?

✎ _____

_____

_____

Since God and His Word are one, what does that say about other religions that teach ideas that are contrary to His Word?

✎ _____

_____

_____

Word Wealth

Word, *logos* (log'-os); Strong's #3056: A transmission of thought, communication, a word of explanation, an utterance, discourse, divine revelation, talk, statement, instruction, an oracle, divine promise, divine doctrine, divine declaration. Jesus is the living *logos*; (John 1:1); the Bible is the written *logos* (Hebrews 4:12); and the Holy Spirit utters the spoken *logos* (1 Corinthians 2:13).

Kingdom Life—*Follow God's Word*

We have just seen that Jesus is *the* Way (John 14:6)—a new and living way (Hebrews 10:20). He is also *the* Word. In John 1:1, 14, we read that God and His Word are one. Jesus Christ is the *logos* of God—communicating, revealing, and declaring God to the world—the Word become flesh.

Just as we follow our Lord Jesus and are led by His Spirit, so we must be led and guided by the Word of God.

The manifold features of God's Word will assist us through life's most practical and difficult circumstances. We read in Psalm 119:105 how God's Word lights our way, giving direction for each step ("to my feet"), and giving wisdom for long-range plans ("to my path"). The regular application of God's Word to life is the most certain way to both success and prosperity in living (Joshua 1:8). God's Word gives wisdom (Psalm 19:7), correction (Proverbs 6:23), and positive, confirming direction. Let God's Word guide, correct, instruct, lead, teach, and confirm. Do not hasten ahead without it—ever!

Read Psalm 119.

Questions:

What does this text reveal in regard to the authority of God's Word in your life?

✎_____

_____

_____

When facing circumstances in life that demand decision or action, do you immediately turn to the Word of God for direction and guidance? Why or why not?

✎_____

_____

_____

_____

In recognizing that Jesus is the Word of God made flesh, what greater understanding do you gain of Him and His ministry through Psalm 119?

✎_____

_____

_____

Behind the Scenes

When Jesus faced Satan's snares in the wilderness (Matthew 4:1–4), He quoted Deuteronomy 8:3: "man shall not live by bread alone, but man lives by every word that proceeds from the mouth of the Lord." The obvious message of both passages is that there is no survival of the soul without God's Word—daily. The fact that the parallel is used in regard to Israel's receiving the daily supply of manna makes clear that a regular, daily portion of God's Word is to be sought and fed upon by the believer.

This is not a matter of legal duty, determining one's salvation, but a matter of personal responsibility, determining one's obedience to the pathway of discipleship. However, let no one suppose spiritual survival is possible for long without nourishment from the Word of God. 1 Peter 2:2 declares that God's Word is as essential to the believer as milk is to a newborn child. But as we come to terms with His Word as key to our survival, let us also see that God has given its pleasantness as a joyful source of sweetness for our living (Psalm 19:10).

Kingdom Life—*Apply the Word of God*

In order to live as people of the covenant—a people in right standing before God and heirs of His promises (Romans 8:17; Galatians 3:29)—we must learn how to apply the power of God's Word into the practicality of life. Subtly, without recognizing it, believers in Jesus Christ have a tendency to make biblical truth *religious* rather than *real*. Yet, it is in the acid test of reality that our faith has the chance to grow and develop. In fact, our loving Heavenly Father will allow real life experiences to come into our lives as divine opportunities for growth. And we will find many occasions when we simply will come to the end of our own resources. It is in these places that we will learn the power of the promises of God's Word.

Read Matthew 4:4; Ephesians 6:10–17.

Questions:

How does the power of God's Word apply to the current situations of your life?

✎ _____

_____

_____

What does it mean that the Word of God is the "sword of the Spirit"?

✎ _____

_____

_____

In what practical ways might you use this "sword of the Spirit" in the challenges of life and against the powers of darkness?

✎ _____

_____

_____

 Kingdom Life—*Use the Sword of the Spirit*

Sooner or later, each of us will face the furnace of life's adversities. In times of trial, temptation, or difficulty, we need to stand on the Word of God. We must wage spiritual warfare and "take the helmet of salvation, and the sword of the Spirit, which is the word of God" (Ephesians 6:17). When Jesus Christ reminded Peter in Luke 22:31, "Simon, Simon! Indeed, Satan has asked for you, that he may sift you as wheat," the Lord was reminding all of us that we have an Adversary. Many of life's trials and problems are brought on by a very real and unseen enemy who wishes to destroy us.

It is the Word of God that is the powerful "sword of the Spirit." In Psalm 119:89 we are told, "Forever, O LORD, Your word is settled in heaven." God's Word is the most powerful force in the universe. We need to apply its power to every area of life. The challenge for us as individual believers in Jesus Christ is to integrate the truth of the Scriptures into the real world and apply the truths of the Bible to everyday life.

Read 1 Peter 4:12–13; Romans 5:3–4; James 1:2–3.

Questions:

How has the truth of the Word of God helped to strengthen you during times of trial?

_____

_____

_____

In what ways do challenges in life help us gain greater insight into God's Word?

_____

_____

_____

What characteristics might God's Word build in us during difficult experiences?

_____

_____

 Kingdom Extra

We have seen that *logos* is the transmission of truth as it is conveyed by God's written Word, through Jesus (the living *Logos*), and by the Holy Spirit's message. This contrasts with the Greek word *rhema*, which is a specific word given or spoken for a specific situation. This recommends that we understand the difference between the entirety of God's revealed Word and the single promise, or promises, the Holy Spirit may bring to our mind from the Word of God.

When facing a situation of need, trial, or difficulty, a promise of God may become a *rhema* to you; that is, a weapon of the Spirit (Ephesians 6:17). Its authority is that this "word" comes from the Bible—God's Word—the completed *logos*. Its immediate significance is that He has "spoken" it to your soul by His Spirit and is calling forth faith. Faith's confession receives God's "words" (*rhema*) and stands firm upon these promises. However, faith's confession does not rest upon human will-power, but upon the divine will revealed in the whole of the Scriptures—the Holy Bible—the *logos* (completed Word) from which the *rhema* (present word of promise) has been received.

Read Romans 10:8, 17.

Questions:

In what specific ways have the promises of God been *rhema* in your life? Write down three promises from God's Word that have given you hope and victory in times of personal trial.

1. _____

2. _____

3. _____

How did the *rhema* of God's Word give you the courage and hope to go on in the midst of difficulty?

_____

_____

_____

Kingdom Life—Access the Power of God's Word

God's Word is total, comprehensive, powerful, and life-changing; it is vital that we read, study, and meditate on it on a daily basis. In Psalm 119:105, we read, "Your Word *is* a lamp to my feet and a light to my path." God's Word is an actual light upon our pathway in life. In Joshua 1:8, we learn that the Word of God holds the secrets to success in life. In order to find that success, there are three ways in which we must interact with the Word of God: we must speak it ("This Book of the Law shall not depart from your mouth"), we must meditate on it ("You shall meditate in it day and night"), and we must do as it says ("Observe to do according to all that is written in it"). Let's look at the power of each interactive element:

Speak God's Word.

Speaking God's Word properly allows for the extension of His kingdom rule in our lives. It is imperative that we speak what the Word of God says about us, the situations we face, and the blessing of the Word to the people we meet. Speaking God's Word should not cause us to become mindless robots, endlessly repeating scriptures, or to become people who glibly attempt to order God around. Nor is the speaking of God's Word supposed to become a kind of Eastern mystical affirmation whereby reality is changed through the constant repetition of a word or idea. The insights of Joshua and the teachings of Jesus both agree: power and authority are released when we speak God's Word with wisdom and grace. When we speak God's Word, a creative force of blessing and power is released.

Like all great truths, it can be perverted and distorted; as in the recent, controversial teachings known by some as "positive confession" or "name it and claim it." Though some may have taken a legitimate biblical truth regarding speaking God's Word and gone off on a tangent, the fact remains that it is the Word of God that commands us to "speak the Word." ("This Book of the Law shall not depart from your mouth.")

Meditate on God's Word.

Unlike Eastern meditation (which encourages emptying of the mind and a general passivity), when the Bible speaks about meditating on the Word of God, it means constantly thinking about a particular passage of Scripture and gleaning all the great truths it contains. In Psalm 119:9–16, the psalmist extols the real, present, and active power of God's Word. He declares that he will "meditate," "contemplate," and "delight" himself in the Word of God. In order to "hide" God's Word in our hearts, we too must seek to engrave its truth on our very souls. God's Word will transform our hearts, minds, and lives as we absorb its truth into our beings. As people of the covenant, it is imperative that we hear the voice of God as He speaks into our lives.

Obey God's Word.

Finally, the power of God's Word is fully released in our lives when we obey and do what the Word of God says. Deuteronomy 28:1 says, "Now it shall come to pass, if you diligently obey the voice of the LORD your God, to observe carefully all His commandments which I command you today, that the LORD your God will set you high above all nations of the earth." What a fantastic promise to those who obey the Word!

Read Mark 11:23; James 1:22–25.

Questions:

What deeper understanding in regard to speaking forth God's Word can you gain from Jesus' words in Mark 11:23?

_____

_____

_____

_____

What happens when we speak negatively or contrary to God's Word in regard to our lives?

_____

_____

_____

According to James 1:22, how is God's Word released and activated in our lives?

_____

_____

_____

Record Your Thoughts

The power of God's Word can be released in our lives. However, we must actively meditate upon what His Word says so that this power can be released.

We can build our faith through reading, hearing, and meditating on the Word of God. Faith that is produced by hearing the Word of God will release God's power in our lives (Romans 10:17). If we would actively meditate on God's Word, we would avoid many of the problems of life. In Psalm 119:92, we read: "Unless Your law had been my delight, I would then have perished in my affliction."

Exercise

Ask yourself, "What afflictions am I perishing from in my life?"

a. spiritual
b. financial
c. physical
d. other

How can you release the power of God's Word into that area of your life through delighting in the Word and meditating in it?

SESSION SEVEN

The Power of Christ's Blood

 Kingdom Key—*Encounter the Lamb of God*

John 1:29 Behold! The Lamb of God who takes away the sin of the world!

The blood of the Lamb of God supernaturally releases us from the dominion and power of Satan's grasp. It has within it enough power to change the course of human history forever. We must learn to think of the blood as more than a red liquid within the body. When it comes to the blood of Christ, there is an actual supernatural property within it that has a power so great that it can transform the very universe. That property of the blood of the Lamb can take people who are in the grip of spiritual and physical death and bring them into eternal life. Praise God!

Read Hebrews 9.

Questions:

At this point in our study, what is your understanding of Jesus as the Lamb of God?

In what way(s) does this truth affect your every day life?

_____

_____

_____

Word Wealth

Sin, *hamartia* (ham-ar-tee'-ah); Strong's #266: Literally "missing the mark," failure, offense, taking the wrong course, wrongdoing, sin, guilt. The New Testament uses the word in generic sense for concrete wrongdoing (John 8:34, 46; 2 Corinthians 11:7; James 1:15); as a principle and quality of action (Romans 5:12, 13, 20; Hebrews 3:13); and as a sinful deed (Matthew 12:31; Acts 7:60; 1 John 5:16).

Behind the Scenes

Read chapters 11 and 12 of Exodus.

In these chapters, we read of the tenth and final plague God visited upon Egypt. In this final visitation, God showed He is not only the controlling force in nature, but is also the controlling force in life and death. God also delivered a death blow to the Egyptians' belief in Osiris, the false god revered by them as the giver of life.

All the firstborn of Egypt, both man and beast, were to die as God Himself brought the plaque upon the land. But God commanded Moses to tell the people of Israel to place the blood of a lamb on the doorposts of their homes as a means of supernatural protection from the death of the firstborn. When the plague descended upon the land, death befell all the firstborn of Egypt, but the people of Israel who obeyed the Word of the Lord were saved.

This sovereign act of God became known as Passover, for the death force literally passed over the people of God. God decreed that this act of protection should be celebrated by a feast as a memorial to those who had been delivered and in commemoration of His presence and protective care.

Passover is celebrated in the month of Nisan (March-April), and marks the new year because its beginning was the beginning of Israel's new life as a separate, autonomous people. It is characterized by the selection of a lamb that is sacrificed four days later and eaten as part of a major commemorative meal. A feast of hope and life, the Passover represents deliverance and new beginnings; in many of its elements, it is a foreshadowing of Christ, our Redeemer, the Lamb of God.

 Kingdom Life—*Apply the Blood of the Lamb*

When a nation, culture, home, or individual walks away from the life-giving principles established by God and chooses to worship the false gods of pleasure, self, and materialism, they also walk away from God's protective covering. Thus death, disease, and destruction are loosed. God does not seek to bring judgment upon us; but just as throwing aside an umbrella in a rainstorm invites being inundated by soaking, pelting rain, those who forsake God's protective covering are prey to natural and supernatural forces that bring destruction.

Divorce, child abuse, AIDS, poverty, drug addiction, alcoholism, sexual immorality, disease, and occult forces seek to ravage and destroy the foundation of our lives, our homes, and our nation. Yet, the blood of the covenant has the supernatural power to stop these forces. The blood of the Lamb has the power to render evil inoperative. Just as the ancient Hebrews applied the blood of a lamb on the doorposts of their homes, so we can apply the blood of the Lamb—Jesus Christ—to the real and present evil that plagues our lives!

The blood of Jesus is powerful. It protects, as in the case of the Passover blood protecting the children of Israel in Egypt. It purges away sin, as in the case of Jesus, the Lamb of God, taking away the sins of the world. And it pulverizes Satan, our enemy, in his attempts to neutralize our testimony to the truth of God's Word in our lives.

The blood of the Lamb is a living, supernatural property that can cleanse us from the most deep-rooted bondages of sin and despair. It has literal wonder-working power to cleanse us from the decay and erosion that sin brings, and bathe us in the pure rejuvenating flow of the Spirit of God. The blood of Jesus Christ binds up shame and despair and releases us to experience the fullness of His glory—the awesome wonder, majesty, and glory of the Lamb upon the throne, the triumphant Christ who brings us before the very throne room of God as children in His heavenly family, to live forever with Him in the splendor of eternity!

Read Exodus 12:13; Hebrews 10:19–21; 1 John 1:7–2:2; Acts 16:31; 2 Chronicles 7:14.

Questions:

Keeping in mind the dynamic truths recorded in Exodus 12:1–7, 12, 13, how can you practically apply the blood of the covenant to your life?

How can you figuratively apply the blood over the doorposts of your home?

How does the blood keep away evil from your dwelling?

How can you appropriate the power of the blood over the lives of your loved ones?

How can you appropriate the power of the blood over the community, city, and nation where you live?

 Kingdom Life—*Set Free by the Blood*

We live in a world contaminated by the death force of sin. This contamination puts our world under the dominion of the god of this age—the enemy of our souls, Satan. The power to resist temptation is dismantled and, without Christ, we find ourselves moving according to the world spirit of this present age. Thus, the world continues to move in a direction that is evil.

However, those who have been washed clean by the blood of Jesus are no longer slaves to sin because the precious life blood of the Lamb of God has set us free from sin's power. John 1:29 says, "The next day John saw Jesus coming toward him, and said, 'Behold! The Lamb of God who takes away the sin of the world!' " Jesus Christ is the very embodiment of the blood of the covenant as the Lamb of God. It is He alone who has the power to remove man's sin through His sacrificial death. Through the blood of the Lamb of God, the power of sin over us is broken and Satan no longer has dominion in our lives. When we lived in spiritual darkness we lived under the rulership of the god of this age. However, when we received Jesus Christ into our lives by faith, we died with Christ and are no longer bound to sin. In the cosmic courts of heaven we have been set free by the power of the blood.

Read Acts 26:18; Colossians 1:12–14; Hebrews 9:11–14; Revelation 12:11.

Questions:

How might you experience the life force activated by the blood of Christ in your day-to-day walk?

The Israelites applied the blood of a lamb to the doorposts of their homes to be delivered from death. What does the term "apply the blood" mean to you in terms of your life and freedom from bondage? How do you "apply the blood?"

_____

_____

_____

Probing the Depths

In Deuteronomy 12:23, in presenting the Law to Moses, God said, "the blood is the life." Just so, the blood of Jesus Christ is a supernatural property that possesses the life force of God Himself. Therefore when His blood was shed for the sins of humankind, the enormous power of God's life force within it was released. Eternal life was activated. Subsequently, the grip of Satan and the powers of darkness are broken as the rejuvenating stream of God's life force is introduced into the human personality. In other words, the bondages and grips of hell's fury are removed as the presence of God within the blood of the Lamb is released.

What the power of the blood means in the most real terms is that the power of Jesus Christ is readily available to anyone who needs it! Thus, when hell's forces are arrayed against us and the fury of demonic forces is at the very worst, the blood makes it possible for us to find salvation, healing, and deliverance. As the blood of the Lamb flows from Calvary into our lives, marriages are restored, victims of abuse are healed, bodies are freed from disease, occult energy is banished, oppression is lifted, and the invading army of God's incredible glory is released into our lives at every dimension.

Kingdom Extra

In prayer, it is common to "plead the blood". Although there is no direct reference to this phrase in the Bible, it is clear that the blood of

Jesus Christ—the blood of the Lamb—has great power in our lives. In Revelation 12:11 Scripture reads, "And they overcame him by the blood of the Lamb and by the word of their testimony." Pleading the blood—applying the power of the blood of Jesus Christ—is simply making use of this divine resource that God has given us. When we apply the blood of Jesus Christ in our lives we are making use of this divine resource by faith.

Record Your Thoughts

How can we, as individuals, apply the power of the blood over our homes? What specific steps must we take to appropriate the blood's power, or plead the blood, over our lives? The following is a suggested prayer exercise in appropriating this power:

Go to God in prayer and appropriate the power of the blood over your home and family. Begin by spending some time in worship and praise before Him. Allow His presence to fill you and His glory to be poured out in your midst.

As a priest and intercessor for your family, your prayer might be something like this: *"Father, in the name of Jesus, I come to You and worship You. I praise Your name, Jesus! God, I come to You, cleansed in the blood of the Lamb. I plead that blood [or, apply the blood] over my home and family. I bind the powers of darkness. In Jesus' name, amen."*

ADDITIONAL OBSERVATIONS

SESSION EIGHT

Entering God's Presence

Hebrews 10:19–22 Therefore, brethren, having boldness to enter the Holiest by the blood of Jesus, by a new and living way which He consecrated for us, through the veil, that is, His flesh, and having a High Priest over the house of God, let us draw near with a true heart in full assurance of faith, having our hearts sprinkled from an evil conscience and our bodies washed with pure water.

In the Book of Exodus, we read of God's command to Moses to employ the artisans and craftsmen of Israel to construct the tabernacle in the wilderness. The tabernacle was more than a place of worship; it is also referred to as the "tent of meeting." It was where God met and interacted with His people in the days following their exodus from Egypt. (To gain greater understanding of the tabernacle and its elements, you may wish to read Exodus 25, 26, and 27.)

The construction and furnishings of the tabernacle are described in detail; each element was symbolic and foreshadowed the ministry of the coming Messiah—God's redemptive plan for man.

For our purposes here, we will focus on two key elements: the Most Holy Place—the place where God's presence dwelt—and the veil (curtain) of separation that hung before it.

In the days of Moses, the manifest presence of God resided within the Most Holy Place—a chamber dedicated to house the Ark of the Covenant. The entrance to the Most Holy Place was secured by a very thick, woven curtain (also called the veil) that some believe was nearly twelve inches thick. No one could go beyond this veil and enter into the presence of God except the High Priest, and he only once per year to offer the sacrifice of Atonement (a blood sacrifice that covered the sins of Israel for one year).

After Israel entered the Promised Land and became a nation, the tabernacle was replaced by the temple, but the construction mirrored that of the tabernacle; the veil of separation still hung before the Most Holy Place.

At the moment Jesus died, "the veil of the temple was torn in two from top to bottom" (Matthew 27:51). The death of Jesus penetrated the separation between God and man and opened the way for each of us to enter into the very presence of God!

Read Hebrews 4:16–5:9; Hebrews 9:1–10:22.

Questions:

What insight do you gain from these verses about Jesus' title as our High Priest?

✎_____

_____

_____

_____

What attitude of heart do you believe is indicated in the words "come boldly before the throne of grace"?

✎_____

_____

_____

What affect does this insight have on your understanding of prayer?

✎_____

_____

_____

_____

What affect does this insight have on your experiential relationship with God?

✎

Word Wealth—*Bold/Boldly*

Bold/boldly, *parrhesia* (par-rhay-see'-ah); Strong's #3954: The root of this Greek word, found in the words *pas* (all) and *rhesis* (speech), denotes freedom of speech or unreserved utterance. It is the absence of fear in speaking boldly and plainly, with confidence, assurance, and cheerful courage.

Kingdom Life—*The Ministry of Christ*

In 1 John 2:1–2, we read: "My little children, these things I write to you, so that you may not sin. And if anyone sins, we have an Advocate with the Father, Jesus Christ the righteous. And He Himself is the propitiation for our sins, and not for ours only but also for the whole world." The power contained in these few words is astounding and world-changing.

Understanding the meaning of the word "propitiation" is key to understanding the full import of these verses. The word translated as "propitiation" is the Greek word *hilasmos* (hil-as-moss') meaning a way whereby sin is covered and erased. It carries the connotation of a satisfied debt—a full reparation. Jesus Christ is our propitiation; by receiving the salvation available through His blood (his death on our behalf) and accepting Him as our Savior and Lord, our sin is completely expunged and the debt of sin (death) has been paid in full on our behalf by the Son of Almighty God.

The word translated as Advocate in this passage is the Greek word *paracletos* (par-ak'-lay-tos), which means one summoned to the aid of another. It also denotes one who is an intercessor, consoler, and comforter. In Romans 8:34, we read that Jesus sits at the Father's right hand,

and "makes intercession for us." The One who gave His life so you might live, the King of kings and Lord of lords, the majestic, risen Lord of all continually upholds, comforts, consoles, and prays for you!

Read Romans 8:34; Hebrews 7:24–27.

Questions:

What affect does the knowledge that Jesus prays for you have on your relationship with Him?

✍ _____

_____

_____

_____

What do you believe the phrase "saved to the uttermost" means?

✍ _____

_____

_____

_____

With these scriptures and what you have read in this study so far in mind, how do you now define the "Good News" of Christ?

✍ _____

_____

_____

_____

Word Wealth

Grace, *charis* (khar'-ece); Strong's #5485: This Greek word is from the same root as *chara*, meaning joy, and *chairo*, meaning to rejoice. *Charis* causes rejoicing. It is the word for God's grace as extended to sinful man. It signifies unmerited favor, undeserved blessing, a free gift.

Probing the Depths

Hebrews 4:16 tells us that we can go boldly to the throne of grace. The gospel of Jesus Christ is called the Good News because through the blood of Jesus Christ we can be cleansed of our sins, shortcomings, mistakes, and failures and come confidently into the presence of Almighty God. The key concept here is the word "grace".

The dynamic of God's grace speaks these truths: 1) God has been reconciled to the world through Christ's sacrifice; 2) we receive unmerited favor and unconditional acceptance from God (Ephesians 1:6); and 3) we are empowered for the tasks we undertake for Him (1 Corinthians 15:10). Taken together, these truths bring believers to a place of genuine freedom where we are free to obey God, not in order to obtain His favor, but because He has already given us His favor. Within His unconditional acceptance given us because of what Christ has done, we are freed from the bondage of focusing on law and our own behavior and loosed into the joy of knowing friendship with Him.

Grace underscores the generosity of God's love, highlighting the truth that God does not coerce change by threatening us; instead He conquers by lavishing His love upon us. His grace frees from wearying, self-generated endeavors and releases us to allow His Holy Spirit within "to will and to do for His good pleasure" (Philippians 2:13).

Read Ephesians 2:4–10.

Questions:

With this in mind, what is your understanding of the term "throne of grace"?

✎ _____

_____

_____

Does grace give us freedom to behave in any way we choose? Why or why not? (Locate Scripture portions to substantiate your answer.)

_____

_____

_____

What importance do our actions or our "works" have in the context of grace?

_____

_____

_____

Now that you have a better understanding of God's grace, what greater insight have you gained in regard to the gift of salvation?

_____

_____

_____

Kingdom Life—*Know God's Unconditional Love*

In our society, we hear the phrase "unconditional love" used constantly, but in the human realm, we never see it practiced. For the most part, human love is dispensed on the basis of how well one measures up or performs. Thus, human love is conditional. As a result, people are placed in a psychological bondage and never feel quite good enough to measure up.

This inability to measure up also affects our relationship to God; we often attempt to alleviate this feeling through doing good things or trying to be spiritual. Yet this is exactly the opposite of what the Bible teaches. It is impossible to earn God's acceptance through actions or behavior. No amount of good works can make a person holy or pure enough to be justified in God's sight.

Fortunately, God has provided a way for us to be totally accepted and loved by Him. It is through the blood of Jesus Christ that God does away with sin. Since our sin is removed by the blood, we can come to

God as a holy and pure being, justified by grace. This truth is revealed in Romans 3:24: "Being justified freely by His grace through the redemption that is in Christ Jesus."

Therefore, God is free to love us *unconditionally* only after the *condition* of sin has been removed through the blood. The same principle follows through in human relationships. Only people who have experienced being loved by God and who have the love of God in them through the Holy Spirit can truly love others. The key truth here is that *God is love.* You cannot remove God from the equation of love and still have love. When the world talks about unconditional love, they always come up empty because they have removed God, who is Love, from the equation.

Read 1 John 4:7–16.

Questions:

Do you experience God's unconditional love in your life? If so, in what way(s)? If not, why do you believe this is so?

_____

_____

_____

In what ways do you attempt to gain God's favor through actions or "works"?

_____

_____

_____

What truths have you understood so far in this study that will allow you to walk freely in the grace of God?

_____

_____

_____

Word Wealth

Love, *agape* (ag-ah'-pay); Strong's #26: Christianity gave new meaning to this Greek word which rarely appears in existing Greek manuscripts from the period. *Agape* denotes an undefeatable benevolence and unconquerable good-will that always seeks the highest good of the other person, no matter whether deserved or undeserved. It is a self-giving love that pours itself out freely without asking anything in return; it does not consider the worth of the one loved. *Agape* is more a love by choice than *philos*, which is love by chance; and it refers to the will rather than the emotions. *Agape* describes the unconditional love God has for the world.

Kingdom Life—*Live Guilt Free*

In our humanistic society, sin is often labeled an antiquated concept because the concept of absolute wrong no longer exists. Along with this denial, an entirely new vocabulary is created in order to justify sin or rationalize it out of existence. For example, a person who commits adultery is having an affair, and homosexuality is called being gay.

Yet, despite all the word games, depression is at an all-time high in our culture. Some philosophers have called this the "Age of Anxiety". The reason for this is that God created humankind as moral beings. When we violate God's laws, we innately feel guilty. Consciences may be hardened and people may appear to not feel any guilt. However, the prevalence of depression, suicide, anxiety (as witnessed by the widespread use of tranquilizers), drugs, and alcohol, suggest that people are not as immune from the effects of sin as they think.

Fortunately, God has given us a path to total freedom and a means of being cleansed of guilt and sin through the blood of Jesus. If we confess our sins to God, we can be set free from the prisons of anxiety, depression, and guilt. However, in order to apply these principles, we must have a firm grasp of what they mean in our lives.

Read 1 Corinthians 6:9–11; 1 John 1:7–10.

Questions:

Are you aware of any sin (actions or attitudes) in your life that may be hindering your walk of faith? If so, take some time now to bring these before the Lord—confess your sin, turn from it, and accept the forgiveness available to you through the power of Jesus' blood.

✎ _____

_____

_____

_____

Are there any feelings of guilt, anxiety, or depression in your life? Ask yourself if they are real and in need of cleansing from the Lord, or if they are vestiges of things already forgiven—cleansed from your life by the blood of the Lamb.

✎ _____

_____

_____

_____

How might you so live your life in the Lord that you avoid any hindrance caused by sin or the power of guilt?

✎ _____

_____

_____

_____

Behind the Scenes

Psychologists recognize that the suppression of unresolved guilt can bring about severe psychological problems. Unforgiveness, resentment, hurt, and woundedness all gnaw at the inner personality. The blood of Jesus Christ brings forgiveness and healing. However, even after forgiveness has been asked of God, many people still live under a dark cloud of condemnation and guilt.

Condemnation and feelings of guilt can produce crippling effects in our lives. They can cause us to question the validity of God's Word, to lose our ability to live secure and confident lives of faith, and so obstruct the flow of God's grace in our lives as to make us ineffective and insecure in our own lives, in prayer, and in ministry to others.

We must realize the difference between conviction and condemnation—between accusation and the work of God's Holy Sprit in our hearts. We learn this difference in the truth of God's mighty Word.

Satan is called "the accuser of our brethren" (Revelation 12:10). He accuses Christians before the throne room of God. But Satan is a liar and the father of lies (John 8:44). His words are perverted and polluted by his hatred of all God loves. He attempts to discredit us before God and undermine us through others, often working through others to bring subtle accusations regarding our motives or character. The purpose of this satanic propaganda campaign is to destroy our effectiveness for Jesus Christ. Satan seeks to condemn us and fill us with debilitating feelings of guilt.

Like all liars, Satan uses grains of truth in his onslaught against God's people. Although our personalities and our behavior may not yet be perfected by the work of God in our lives, we are under grace and not the Law. We have been cleansed by the blood of the Lamb. Our righteousness is not in and of ourselves, but our righteousness is in Christ. God views us as totally sinless and pure through the blood of Jesus Christ. Therefore, as we grow as believers, we never have to feel condemned or accused, because the blood of Jesus Christ cleanses us from all sin.

When we understand what the blood of Jesus Christ does for us, we never have to be victimized again by Satan's dark strategy. There may be places in our lives where repentance and confession of sin are necessary. We may have to choose to turn away from sin and walk the paths of righteousness. This drawing away from sin and toward God is a result of the Holy Spirit at work in our hearts and lives—convicting us of the sin that separates us from our Father. Rather than debilitating our faith, this act of the Holy Spirit enlivens us and renews our faith if we but surrender to His prompting and repent of our sin.

Read Romans 7:9–8:1.

Questions:

What is your understanding of the conflict Paul experienced?

_____

_____

_____

In your own words, what is the difference between conviction and condemnation?

_____

_____

How has each of these come into play in your own walk of faith?

_____

_____

Which do you believe Paul experienced in the passage from Romans? What was his reaction?

_____

_____

_____

What truth can you glean from this session and from the Romans passage that will enable you to live free from guilt and condemnation?

_____

_____

_____

Behind the Scenes

One of the laws of physics is that anything in motion causes friction. Similarly, one of the laws of the spiritual realm is that any motion or progress in the pursuit of godliness will produce friction as it confronts the carnality of our human nature. In Paul's pursuit of godly living, note his as evidenced when he writes, "I will to do." To exercise the will is to determine or choose or commit to do something. In Paul's case, he "wills" to do good, that is, to resist the flesh's natural drift toward the unworthy, immoral, or self-serving. Note also the conflict: "even is present," that is, there is no escape from human inclinations, except through the abiding presence of the Holy Spirit (Romans 7:24—8:4).

The call is to commit to godliness with relentless persistence. There is a higher law that assures victory as we overcome the friction of the flesh, pressing forward in the determined, passionate pursuit of Christ.

Record Your Thoughts

It is vitally important that, as believers in Jesus Christ, we recognize the traps and strategies that Satan will attempt to use against us. In Ephesians 6:11 we are admonished: "Put on the whole armor of God, that you may be able to stand against the wiles of the Devil." In Genesis 3:1 we read, "Now the serpent was more cunning than any beast of the field which the LORD God had made."

We must recognize that condemnation and accusation are two of the Devil's prime strategies in attempting to destroy our effectiveness in Jesus Christ.

Furthermore, we must understand the patterns he uses in his schemes against us. Once we recognize the satanic game plan, then we can learn to apply the blood of Jesus Christ more effectively.

After prayerful consideration, identify areas in which you have been tempted to sin and feel condemned in a kind of vicious cycle or treadmill experience. What do you see as the solution?

As you list these areas, remember that you are in Christ and in Him there is no condemnation. Because of Him, you can boldly enter into God's presence. Your righteousness is in Christ and, because of Him, you are forgiven the moment you ask. Through Him you are freed from the bondage of guilt and shame and enabled to walk in victory as you love and serve the Lord.

SESSION NINE

The Fruit of God's Word

John 15:7–8 If you abide in Me, and My words abide in you, you will ask what you desire, and it shall be done for you. By this My Father is glorified, that you bear much fruit; so you will be My disciples.

The primary Greek word translated "abide" (*meno*; Strong's #3306) means to stay. Whether in regard to a given place, state, relationship, or state of expectancy, it communicates the idea of staying in place, remaining steadfast, continuing persistently, or continually living within. The model is that of Jesus Christ and the Holy Spirit who, "descending from heaven like a dove . . . remained [*meno*] upon Him" (John 1:32).

We are called to abide in Christ and to allow His Word to abide in us. This abiding should have as its pattern the relationship or connectedness that exists between Christ and the Holy Spirit. A steadfast, persistent, continual connection should be firmly established within us whereby our abiding in Christ and His Word in us should be as closely linked to our being as our very breath.

Earlier in this passage from John, Jesus refers to Himself as the "true vine" and to us as branches (John 15:1–6). This analogy clearly demonstrates the inextricable nature of our abiding—if we are cut off from Christ, the true vine, we cannot live. However, when we enjoy the utter connectedness of abiding in the Vine, with His life flowing through us, we not only know life, but fruitful, abundant life.

Knowing the Word to the point where it flows as freely as breath and is a continual "voice" within you, is the key to living a fruitful life to the glory of God.

Read John 17:20–23.

Questions:

We read in John 17, a prayer Jesus prayed just before He was crucified; that prayer was for us—those who would believe. In what way is this prayer linked to Christ's teaching about the vine?

_____

_____

_____

What does it mean to be "one" with Christ?

_____

_____

_____

In what ways should our abiding connectedness with Him result in greater fruitfulness in our lives?

_____

_____

_____

Kingdom Life—*Feed on God's Word*

In 1 Peter 2:2, we read that we should "as newborn babes, desire the pure milk of the word, that you may grow thereby". Just as a newborn child requires regular feeding, so we must regularly feed on the Word of God. Just as a newborn infant's desire for milk is all-encompassing and even desperate, sometimes causing the child's need to be heard by all, so should our desire be for the Word of God.

However, infants grow and their dietary needs change. Where milk once sufficed, a growing child needs solid food to insure physical health. Scripture presents this as an analogy of our growth in Christ. Newborn babies in Christ must have regular feedings of the milk of the

Word of God to grow and stay spiritually healthy. When people mature in Christ, they must have the solid food (meat) of the Word. Hebrews 5:12–14 illustrates this principle.

In 1 Corinthians 3:1–3, the apostle Paul states that envy, strife, and divisions are evidence of spiritual immaturity and carnality. Tragically, a great deal of spiritual immaturity is seen in the church today: envy, strife, and divisions. This is because many Christians are babes in Christ—still feeding on the milk of the Word and not on solid food. They are behaving like babies and not mature people of God. When we eat of the solid food of the Word, we are transformed by its power (Psalm 19:7). We begin to see ourselves in Christ, and our eternal destiny begins to unfold in our hearts and in our lives.

Read Psalm 119.

Questions:

What adjectives or descriptive phrases can you find that characterize the work of the Word in our lives? List them here.

_____

_____

_____

What evidence do you see in your own life that confirms you are maturing in your faith walk?

_____

_____

_____

What steps can you take to increase your intake of God's Word? How can you insure you make what you learn an active part of your life?

_____

_____

_____

Kingdom Life—*Produce Godly Fruit*

In John 15:1–16, Jesus repeatedly speaks of bearing "fruit." Often, when we think of the "fruit" in the life of a believer, we think of behavior or godly works. But the fruit that God—the heavenly vinedresser—looks for in His people is Christlikeness (see Galatians 5:22–23).

The goal for a follower of Jesus is to walk in both the power and the character of the kingdom. God made His power and authority available to produce a different kind of lifestyle in the believer—one that attracts others by its light in contrast to the darkness of the world. The manifestation of this light in our lives is displayed through the godly characteristics of Jesus as imparted to us by the Holy Spirit. These are listed in Galatians 5:22–23: love, joy, peace, longsuffering, kindness, goodness, faithfulness, gentleness, and self-control. While a believer may be a channel through which God touches man with the miraculous, we should not perceive that empowerment as fruit. Though one may be used by God to reach thousands for the Lord, or create beauty in His name, these are not the fruit God seeks in the lives of those in His kingdom. Only the Holy Spirit can produce fruit in our lives; our own efforts can never do so.

It is interesting to note that the first three "fruit" in the list from Galatians are: love, joy, and peace. These concern our attitude toward God. The second three: longsuffering, kindness, and goodness, deal with social relationships. And the third group: faithfulness, gentleness, and self-control, guide our conduct as people of the Covenant—the children of God.

Read Ephesians 5:8–16; James 3:17–18.

Questions:

What is the "fruit of righteousness"?

✎

Does this mean the works done for God are not of value? Give a scriptural foundation for your answer.

✎ _____

_____

_____

With this section in mind, what do you see as the fruit in your own life?

✎ _____

_____

_____

In what way can you increase the fruit of the Spirit in your life?

✎ _____

_____

_____

Behind the Scenes

God's Word can produce purpose and power in our lives; it can reveal and enable our destinies. However, it is obvious to any observer that today's world is severely lacking in any true vision or purpose. Life around us seems to be lived on impulse and without consideration of any overriding purpose of more import than immediate, personal gratification.

Proverbs 29:18 says, "Where there is no revelation, the people cast off restraint." The Old Testament word translated here as "revelation" is *chizzayown* (khiz-zaw-yone'), which means a revelation, especially via a dream; in many translations the word is translated as "vision." Therefore, what this scripture tells us is that life lived without purpose and without divine revelation of truth is a life headed toward destruction.

As you discovered in your review of Psalm 119, the entrance of God's Word into the human heart brings undreamed-of fulfillment, purpose, and destiny. The thief (Satan) wants to steal, kill, and destroy that purpose, so the forces of hell have an all-out strategy to block God's Word from the lives of people. They want to so blind the hearts of men so as to prevent the Word of God from taking root, growing, and bearing fruit in the lives of God's people.

Read Mark 4:13–20.

Questions:

What is the "vision" that determines your course in life? Is that "vision" consistent with God's will in your life?

_____

_____

_____

What "cares of this world" threaten to choke the Word from your life?

_____

_____

_____

What steps can you take to prepare "good ground" within you in which God's Word can thrive?

_____

_____

_____

 ## Kingdom Life—Be Changed by the Word

The power of God's Word is like a seed that is able to refine, purify and change us into God's own image. It will take deep root in our souls and transform us from within. In James 1:21, we read that the implanted Word is able to save our souls. The word translated as "souls" is the Greek word *psuche*

(psoo-khay'). It means the seat of affections, will, desire, emotions, mind, reason, and understanding—the inner self or the essence of life.

When the Bible states that the implanted Word can save our souls, it means that the power of God's Word can change us as people. The Word of God can penetrate the depths of our will, desire, emotions, reason, and memory. The Word transforms us into what Christ wants us to be. The implanted Word can bring the healing power of God's Word into the very center of our being and set us free at the deepest dimensions. The implanted Word can enter us at the depths of our humanity and deliver us from fear, insecurity, addictions, bondage, oppression, and any form of darkness. The implanted Word can literally rescue us from life's prisons and bring us into the kingdom of light and joy for all eternity.

Read John 1:1–13; 1 John 1:5–7; James 1:17–25.

Questions:

How are the "light" spoken of in these verses and the Word of God related?

According to what you have learned thus far in this study, what is the agent that has brought you out of darkness and into the marvelous kingdom of God's light?

How can you apply the truth of James 1:22–25 to your life?

What steps can you take to discern God's direction in your life? How is this knowledge like a light? (See Psalm 119:105.)

✎ _____

_____

_____

 Kingdom Life—*Reflect Christ*

Take another look at James 1:21–25. God's Word is "the perfect law of liberty." It does not enslave us to the bondage of legalism, but frees us to keep its precepts by the inner prompting and enabling of the Spirit. This text shows the Word of God as a means of reflection—a mirror into which we are to look and see ourselves. In this passage, we see the call to purity—to a quest, not so much to perfection as to liberation from those things that may inhibit effectiveness and reduce power-filled living.

When we look into "the perfect law of liberty," the light of God's Word purifies us and calls us to allow the implanted Word to conform us into the image of Jesus Christ. Reading the Word of God is like looking into a supernatural mirror. However, it is unlike any earthly mirror. It not only has the capacity of showing us what we look like spiritually, but it also contains the power to change our very image or reflection into the image of Christ.

Read 1 Corinthians 13:12; 2 Corinthians 3:18.

Questions:

In what ways do you see your image and the image of Christ connected?

✎ _____

_____

_____

_____

In considering that Jesus is the Vine and you are a branch on that Vine, what further meaning can you draw from the mirror analogy contained in the referenced verses of this section?

In what way is being a "doer" of the Word living out the call to abide in Christ?

How might you increase your effectiveness in showing forth the image of Christ to the world?

Record Your Thoughts

The Bible teaches us that it is important to be a doer of the Word and not just a hearer (James 1:22). After prayerful consideration, determine five areas in which you personally need to both hear and do what the Word of God says. Write them below and include references to Bible verses that support your feeling.

ADDITIONAL OBSERVATIONS

SESSION TEN

Communion With and Through Christ

 Kingdom Key—*Receive of His Life*

John 6:56–57 He who eats My flesh and drinks My blood abides in Me, and I in him. As the living Father sent Me, and I live because of the Father, so he who feeds on Me will live because of Me.

In Session One of this study, we explored the power of the blood in the remission of sin. We learned that we are set free from the bondage of sin through the covenant in Christ's blood—the sacrificial death of the Son of God satisfied for eternity the requirements of a holy God.

In this passage, Jesus brings an even greater understanding of His sacrifice and the life He gave for the salvation of the world. Yet, those who followed Him were appalled at the concept of partaking of the very flesh and blood of Jesus. Many "walked with Him no more" because they did not understand the spiritual implications of Jesus' words (John 6:66).

These confused and horrified disciples mistakenly heard meaning behind Jesus' words that caused them great distress. They knew God's Word concerning Old Testament sacrifice and understood that the life of the flesh is in the blood (Leviticus 17:11). According to the Word of God, the blood represents the life-force of the living soul (Genesis 4:10; 9:4–6; Deuteronomy 12:23). The Word of God strictly prohibited the eating of blood. In addition, they knew pagan worship often incorporated the ritual drinking of blood, believing the participant captured the life-force of a creature by consuming its blood.

But Jesus' words are to be understood spiritually. His words point to the violent death He would suffer and the necessity of all men to receive the benefits of His death by coming to Him and believing in Him. Although we need not see in this verse the directive to receive the Eucharist in order to obtain salvation, we do learn the very vital importance of Communion in strengthening our souls, inviting the flow of healing into our lives, and for testifying to our faith.

Read 1 Corinthians 11:23–30.

Questions:

In what ways do you believe the observance of Communion holds power in our lives?

✎ _____

_____

_____

_____

In 1 Corinthians 11:27, Paul warns against receiving the Lord's Supper in an unworthy manner. What do you believe is a worthy manner?

✎ _____

_____

_____

_____

The church is referred to as the body of Christ (Ephesians 5:30). What connection do you see between this passage in 1 Corinthians and the truth that we are all members of the body of Christ?

✎ _____

_____

_____

_____

Kingdom Life—*Life through the Blood*

The bondage of sin that Adam and Eve unleashed upon the human race by disobeying the Word of God in the Garden of Eden was undone by the power of Christ's blood. When Jesus Christ said, "This cup *is* the new covenant in My blood, which is shed for you" (Luke 22:20), He was explaining that, through the shedding of His blood, we can experience release from the bondage of sin and freedom from captivity to Satan's dominion.

The blood of Jesus Christ has destroyed the power of sin, death, and the authority of Satan over humankind. The blood of Jesus Christ is the most powerful force on this earth. The blood of Jesus Christ is the Word of God energized and active in redeeming humankind from the death force that Adam and Eve passed on through the generations. It literally removes the power of sin and infuses individuals with God's very eternal nature, once again. The blood of Jesus Christ acts like a heavenly transfusion, where the contaminated blood, infected with the death force, is removed. The very life of God Himself is reintroduced into the human system through the blood of Jesus Christ.

The Lord's Supper, or Communion, is not merely a religious ritual. It is communion in the literal sense of the word. We experience supernatural communion with the living God because of the blood of Jesus. Awesome power, wonder, and majesty are released when we, as ordinary people, can be lifted into the presence of the Infinite One through the blood of Jesus Christ.

Read Luke 22.

Questions:

What is your attitude when you receive communion? Is it a time of sober reflection or joyful anticipation? Why?

✎ _____

_____

_____

In what ways do you see Satan attempting to diffuse your experience with or cause you to deny the power of the blood in your life?

✎_____

_____

_____

How do you see Satan making the same efforts in the world around you?

✎_____

_____

_____

What steps can you take to abide with the knowledge and power of the blood at work in your life?

✎_____

_____

_____

 Probing the Depths

Many of Jesus' actions and words at the Last Supper, such as the breaking and distributing of the bread, were part of the prescribed Passover ritual. But when Jesus said, "This is My body" and "This is My blood" while distributing the bread and the cup, He did something totally new. These words, which were intended for our blessing, have been the focus of sharp disagreement among Christians for centuries. In what sense are the bread and wine Christ's body and blood? What should the Lord's Supper mean to us? The answers to these questions are often grouped into four categories, although there are variations within these four broad views.

The transubstantiation view. The first view is that of the Roman Catholic Church (especially before the Second Vatican Council of 1962–1965). This view holds that the bread and wine become the actual body and blood of Christ when the words of institution are spoken by the priest. This doctrine holds that while the physical properties (taste, appearance, etc.) of the bread and wine do not change, the inner reality of these elements undergoes a spiritual change.

While this view may help to foster a serious attitude toward the Eucharist, it fails to grasp the figurative nature of Jesus' language. He probably meant, "This bread represents My body" and "This wine represents My blood." Jesus often used figurative language (Luke 8:11, 21).

The consubstantiation view. The second viewpoint, developed by Martin Luther, is that Christ's body and blood are truly present "in, with, and under" the bread and wine. The elements do not actually change into Christ's body and blood. But in the same way that heat is present in a piece of hot iron, so Christ is present in the elements.

This position can encourage the recipient of the Eucharist with the realization that Christ is actually present at the Supper. But it also misses the figurative use of Jesus' words. It also may tend to draw more attention to the bread and wine than to Christ Himself.

The symbolic view. Also known as the memorial view, the position is derived from the teachings of the Swiss reformer, Ulrich Zwingli. Although his teaching is not completely clear, he basically held that the bread and wine were only symbols of the sacrificed body and blood of Christ. He taught that the Lord's Supper is primarily a memorial ceremony of Christ's finished work, but that it is also to be an occasion when God's people pledge their unity with one another and their loyalty to Christ. This is the viewpoint held by most Baptist and independent churches. While Zwingli's ideas are basically sound, this position tends to place more emphasis on the Christian than on Christ.

The dynamic view. This view was developed by John Calvin and the Reformed and Presbyterian churches that follow his teachings. Also known as the spiritual presence view, it stands somewhere between the positions of Luther and Zwingli.

Calvin agreed with Zwingli that the bread and wine are to be understood symbolically. Christ is not physically present in the elements, because His risen, glorified body is in heaven (Hebrews 10:12–13). Still, He is dynamically and spiritually present in the Lord's Supper through the Holy Spirit.

In the worship service (but not at any one precise moment), when the Word of God is proclaimed and the Lord's Supper is received, the glorified Christ actually gives spiritual nourishment from His own glorified body to those who receive it. As bread nourishes the physical body, so Christ's glorified body enlivens the soul. Because of the organic union between Christ, the risen Head, and the members of His body, the church (Ephesians 1:18–23; 4:15–16; 5:23), this nourishment is conveyed to Christians by the Spirit who dwells in them (Romans 8:9–11). Calvin admits that the way the Spirit does this is a genuine mystery. Yet, it is not contrary to reason—simply above reason.

Calvin seemed at times to place more emphasis on Jesus' glorified flesh and blood than the Scripture's focus, but his position helps to explain why the Eucharist is so important for the Christian to observe and why it is such a serious offense to misuse it. His view also corresponds well with those Scriptures that speak of God's nourishing and empowering work in His people (Ephesians 3:14–21; Colossians 2:6–10, 19).

Word Wealth

Thanks, *euchasristeo* (yoo-khar-is-the'-oh); Strong's #2168: Greek word formed from *eu*, meaning well, and *chariozomai*, meaning to give freely. It means to be grateful, to express gratitude, to be thankful. Eleven of the thirty-nine appearances of the word in the New Testament refer to partaking of the Lord's Supper, while twenty-eight occurrences describe the praise words given to the Godhead. During the second century, Eucharist became the generic term for the Lord's Supper.

Kingdom Life—*Give Thanks for the Blood of Christ*

In partaking of the blood of the New Covenant, it is important that we understand the full scope of communion in our lives. Let us explore five principles that outline the full scope of communion.

1. Communion Is a Celebration of Victory

Read Revelation 12:10–11.

Communion is a celebration of the New Covenant. Christ won the victory over Satan for us. Although many churches still take communion in a morose sense, the spirit of communion is a triumphant and victorious one in which we are to be reminded that Jesus Christ conquered the power of the enemy! Jesus Christ told us to drink of the cup of the blood of the New Covenant and to "do this in remembrance of Me." We are to remember that Jesus Christ is the Lamb of God whose blood redeemed us from the power of sin and death and set us free from the dominion of Satan.

2. Communion Is a Proclamation of Redemption

Read 1 Corinthians 11:26.

When we take communion, we are to take it as a proclamation of redemption. The only way God could redeem humankind was through the blood of Jesus Christ. Humankind was in need of a Redeemer, and redemption demands a price be paid. Every time we come to the Lord's Table, our hearts should be filled with gratitude as we recall the price Jesus paid to free us. He is our Redeemer and in Him we have victory over sin and death.

3. Communion Is a Declaration of Dependence

Read John 6:53.

When we take communion, we are declaring our total dependence upon Jesus Christ and His power. As we surrender to His lordship and depend upon Him for our strength, partaking of His body and blood, the dynamism of the Holy Spirit is released in us. The New Covenant releases supernatural energy into our lives through the blood of Jesus Christ.

4. Communion Is an Examination of Self

Read 1 Corinthians 11:28–29.

Although communion is not to be a morose ritual, it is a time when we are to search our own hearts in the presence of God and ask to be cleansed from our sins through the blood of Jesus Christ.

This particular passage of scripture is often misunderstood and used as a means of condemnation. However, the purpose of this scripture is to teach us to become true disciples who accept the discipline that discipleship brings. Thus we examine ourselves in the light of the Holy Spirit, allowing God's Spirit to point out areas of disobedience in our lives. It is here that we take advantage of the blessing that the New Covenant brings: the complete forgiveness of sins through the blood of Jesus Christ. We must realize that all of us will sin as we walk with Christ in this life. Wrong attitudes, living in fear instead of faith, anger, jealousy, and deliberate sins must all be confessed before the Lord, so we can receive healing, cleansing, and deliverance. Sin brings bondage into our lives and can actually prevent the full release of our potential in the Lord.

5. Communion Is a Reception of Provision
   Read John 10:7–15.
   The purpose of the blood of the New Covenant is that Jesus Christ paid not only for our sins, but for the full provision for every need in our lives—to bring us abundant life. To take the Lord's Supper in an unworthy manner is to limit, by our unbelief, the full provision of what God has done. The New Covenant was made available to us by the price of Christ's blood and His death on the Cross. It provides healing, provision of physical needs, peace of mind, deliverance, freedom from fear, and spiritual power and purpose. When we take communion, we are to believe that Jesus Christ's blood made it possible for us to receive the full worth of God's unlimited provision in every area of our lives! The awesome reality of this total provision, made possible by the blood of the covenant, should revolutionize our understanding of how good God is and how this goodness can be manifest in every area of our lives.
   Read 1 John 5:11–20.

Questions:

What provisions has God assured you through the victory of Jesus over Satan's dominion?

✎ _____

_____

_____

Do you experience God's total provision in your life? If not, what need do you lack?

✎ _____

_____

_____

What can block the flow of God's provision in your life?

✎ _____

_____

_____

What Scripture portions can you locate that promise you the provision you lack?

✎ _____

_____

_____

How can you open the way to receive those things promised by God that you currently lack?

✎ _____

_____

_____

_____

Record Your Thoughts

In the exercise below, apply the power and reality of what Christ meant when He said, "Do this in remembrance of Me." Although communion is best taken with other believers in a corporate setting, its wonder and power can be released privately with the Lord. Simply take some bread and grape juice in the privacy of your home or office and go to God in prayer. Begin by praising Him, worshiping Him, and thanking Him in a celebration of victory.

Go to God in a proclamation of redemption. Thank Him for His death upon the Cross. Declare your dependence upon Him as you eat of the bread and drink the juice, which is the blood of the New Covenant poured out for you. Ask Him to forgive you and cleanse you by the blood of the Lamb. Allow yourself to be cleansed, refreshed, and delivered by the blood of the New Covenant. Praise the Lord, and thank Him for His forgiveness.

Finally, receive the full provision of the Lord by faith. Ask Him in full confidence, specifically, for your needs or the needs of others. The blood of the covenant releases God's full provisions for whatever you need.

In your time of prayer, with thanksgiving, remember how God has performed miracles of provision for you in the past. Rejoice and praise Him for those miracles. Allow the reminder of past provisions to strengthen your heart for present situations as you receive into your being the elements of Communion—joining in unity with your Redeemer in His life, death, and resurrection.

SESSION ELEVEN

Power for Daily Living

 Kingdom Key—*Receive the Provision of the Word*

Matthew 16:19 And I will give you the keys of the kingdom of heaven, and whatever you bind on earth will be bound in heaven, and whatever you loose on earth will be loosed in heaven.

These were Jesus' words to Peter following his declaration that Jesus is "the Christ, the Son of the living God." To fully understand Jesus' meaning, it is necessary to look to the Greek words used in the preceding verses: "Blessed are you, Simon Bar-Jonah, for flesh and blood has not revealed *this* to you, but My Father who is in heaven. And I also say to you that you are Peter, and on this rock I will build My church, and the gates of Hades shall not prevail against it."

In this passage, Jesus calls Simon by the name Peter (*petros*), meaning a stone or a piece of rock. Elsewhere in Scripture, the Lord is called the Rock (as in Psalm 61:2, 89:26, 95:1; 1 Corinthians 10:4). In speaking of the "rock" upon which He will build the church, Jesus uses the word *petra*, meaning foundation rock or boulder—that Rock is Jesus. In Jesus' strong proclamation, He may have meant that, while the church is built upon Him (*Petra*), the structure is built out of those stones (*petros*) that partake of His nature—those who become the people of the New Covenant through their confession of faith. Peter, therefore, was the first of many stones (*petros*) from which the Lord builds His church (1 Peter 2:4–5).

The "keys" of which Jesus spoke denote authority. Through Peter, a representative of the church throughout the ages, Jesus passed on to His church His authority to bind and to loose on earth. The terms "bind" and "loose" have to do with forbidding or permitting. Such authority is seen in the believers' ability to "loose" those who are bound by sin through preaching the provision of freedom from sin in Jesus. The church can "bind" demonic oppression or possession in the name of Jesus. Jesus is the One who has activated these provisions through His Cross; He charged the church with the implementation of what He released through His life, death, and resurrection. As we read in 2 Corinthians 4:7, within the frail and fragile vessels of our lives, we hold untold treasure—the very life and authority of our Lord.

Read 2 Corinthians 4.

Questions:

When have you experienced the afflictions and despair of which this passage speaks?

✎ _____

_____

How might walking in the authority of Jesus in the ability to bind and loose have altered your experience(s)?

✎ _____

_____

What is your current understanding of the "light" spoken of in verse 6 of this passage?

✎ _____

_____

_____

Kingdom Life—Receive the Light of God

Read Colossians 1:9–14.

Paul reminds us that we have been rescued from the tyranny of darkness and are now qualified to be "partakers of the inheritance of the saints in the light." But we must walk worthy of that high calling. Paul begs those who love the Lord to walk with a radical commitment of will, affection, and disposition to pleasing Christ—a walk of fruitfulness, growth in godly knowledge, divine empowerment, and thankfulness. Since God has delivered us from darkness, we must now live as a people alive within the light of God.

According to Psalm 119:105, God's Word is light; and verse 130 tells us that when we receive God's Word, we receive its light within ourselves. The light of the Word brings wisdom, understanding, joy, peace, and freedom (Psalm 119); it changes our very nature. We are changed by the power of the Word.

Further, we understand from Jesus' words in Matthew 5:16, that our lives—our choices, actions, and behaviors—are to please our Father and reflect the light of God to a world lost in the darkness of Satan's cruel bondage. The light of the kingdom should so overflow from us as to change the world around us. To be filled with the light of the kingdom, we must be filled with the Word of God.

Read Matthew 5:14–16; 1 John 1:5–9.

Questions:

In what ways is the light of God reflected in your life?

In what ways do you often fail to reflect His light?

Are you so filled with the Word of God that it overflows to the world around you? Why do you believe this is so?

What practical steps can you take to increase the flow of "light" in and through your life?

_____

_____

_____

Kingdom Life—*Realize Your Inheritance*

An inheritance is the passing of wealth, property, titles, and rights to another upon the death of an individual. We often hear brothers and sisters in the faith refer to the inheritance we have through Christ Jesus. However, it will be of great benefit to explore here the specifics of our inheritance.

In Galatians 3:29, we learn that if we belong to Christ, "then [we] are Abraham's seed, and heirs according to the promise." We know from Old and New Testament accounts, that Abraham is the prototype of all who experience God's process of redemption, first and foremost, in his relationship to God by faith. Abraham is also shown as a case of God's program to recover man's "reign in life" (Romans 5:17). As such, he is God's example of His plan to establish His kingdom's rule in all the Earth through the people of His covenant. God declared His plan to beget innumerable children modeled after this prototypical father of faith (Romans 4:11). This truth is confirmed in Romans 4:13, where Abraham's designation as "heir of the world" parallels Jesus' promise that His followers, who humble themselves in faith, shall also be recipients of "the kingdom" and shall "inherit the earth" (Matthew 5:3–5).

God's words and dealings in the life of Abraham reveal that His unfolding program of redemption is dual: (1) restoring relationship *to* God to establish fellowship with Him and (2) restoring rulership in life *under* God to reestablish human ability to rule in life's practical details of family and business. Thus, under His covenant, God promised Abraham both *progeny*—a family line—and *property*—an economic base. This illustrates God's progressive processing of His redemptive promise. He not only provides for restored fellowship with Himself (relationship), but covenants for human fulfillment and personal fruitfulness in life. This plan is geared not only to bless His people, but to make them a blessing to others.

Thus, our inheritance in God's kingdom *is* God's kingdom—we operate in His name, His power has been given to us through the Holy Spirit, and He has granted us entrance and dwelling (John 14:2–3) within His eternal home.

Read Romans 8:1–17; Galatians 4:1–7; Hebrews 1–2.

Questions:

What are the benefits of being an heir of the promise?

In what ways do you currently enjoy the inheritance that is yours through Christ?

What are the responsibilities of being an heir of the promise?

In what ways do you currently discharge those responsibilities?

Kingdom Life—*Possess the Promises*

Not only does God's Word purify our lives and lead us to salvation in Christ, but God's Word also makes it possible for us to unlock supernatural provisions here on earth. In Matthew 6:25–34, Jesus teaches that we are not to worry about the things we need to exist in this life. Our Heavenly Father will meet all of our needs through the power of His Word. In Matthew 16:19, we read that Jesus Christ has given us the keys of His kingdom so that whatever we ask, He will do it for us (Matthew 18:18–19).

God has given us the keys of His kingdom to unlock supernatural provisions for our lives by the power of His Word. If we read the Word of God and understand its promises for our lives, then we can boldly face the future in the confidence that those promises cover every situation and circumstance we could possibly face. Our responsibility is to know what God's Word says and to ask Him for what we need. We can overcome in this life if we take full advantage of the supernatural provisions He has made available to us in Christ (Philippians 4:19).

God is intimately concerned with every aspect of our lives—our spiritual well-being, as well as our daily lives. Unfortunately, many of us have a tendency to over-spiritualize the meaning of the word "salvation" and divorce it from the practical issues of life. But this is not what the Bible teaches. God is not only concerned with our eternal salvation, He is also concerned about our total well-being here on earth.

Read Matthew 6:25–34; John 14:13–14, 15:15–16, 16:24–27.

Questions:

In what ways do you see concern about tomorrow being a guiding force in the lives of the ones around you? In your own life?

✎ _____

_____

_____

_____

In 1 John 2:16, we learn the spirit of the world is consumed by: "the lust of the flesh, the lust of the eyes, and the pride of life." In what ways do these sinful attitudes shape the world in which we live?

✎ _____

_____

Are there areas of your own life ruled by any of these sinful attitudes?

✎ _____

_____

What practical steps can you take to turn from these attitudes and begin to more fully walk in the light of God's Word?

✎ _____

_____

If you give priority to seeking God's kingdom, what do you believe will be the result in your life?

✎ _____

_____

Word Wealth

Salvation, *soteria* (so-tay-ree'-ah); Strong's #4991: This Greek word means deliverance, preservation, soundness, prosperity, happiness, rescue, and/or general well-being. The word is used in the New Testament in both a material, temporal sense, and in a spiritual, eternal one. *Soteria* is especially used to mean spiritual well-being. Salvation is a present possession (2 Corinthians 1:6, 7:10) with a fuller realization in the future (Romans 13:11, 1 Thessalonians 5:8–9).

Clearly, salvation covers life in the here and now, as well as life in the hereafter. Understanding and appropriating the promises of God's Word by faith help us to overcome and live victoriously here on earth.

Record Your Thoughts

Based on Psalm 119:11 and Psalm 119:9, if you hide God's Word in your heart and take heed to its counsel, then your paths will be made straight in life.

The following exercise will enable you to utilize this truth on a practical level. On the left side, list a temptation, wrong attitude, or sin in your own life. On the right side, write down a promise or commandment that will help you overcome.

Unbiblical Life Response

Example: Fear

Scriptural Answer

2 Timothy 1:7
"For God has not given us a spirit of fear, but of power and of love and of a sound mind."

Now take each of the problem areas of your life before God. Allow Him to bring the light of His Word to bear on each of these areas of darkness in your life. Ask Him to cleanse you from sin and fill you with the light of life. Begin today to walk as one who has been promised an eternal inheritance by Almighty God.

SESSION TWELVE

Power Over the Enemy

Kingdom Key—*Overcome Satan*

Revelation 12:10–11 Then I heard a loud voice saying in heaven, "Now salvation, and strength, and the kingdom of our God, and the power of His Christ have come, for the accuser of our brethren, who accused them before our God day and night, has been cast down. And they overcame him by the blood of the Lamb and by the word of their testimony, and they did not love their lives to the death.

Revelation 12:11 tells us that we overcome Satan by the blood of the Lamb and the word of our testimony. This Bible verse outlines the fact that we are in a great cosmic struggle with Satan; but it is a battle in which we will be victorious. We will overcome by appropriating the finished work of Christ and by the public confession of our faith. To overcome, we must maintain a constant posture under the authority of Christ's victory through the cross and through steadfastness to the promise and authority of God's Word.

Through Christ's redemptive work in our lives, we can silence Satan's attempts to intimidate us. His accusing voice of condemnation and guilt is swallowed up in the triumph of Calvary.

Declare your abiding faith in the accomplished work of the cross, and constantly participate in Jesus' ultimate victory. You can overcome Satan in your own life if you hold fast to the power of the cross, speaking your confession of faith through your words, attitudes, and actions.

Read Revelation 2:7, 11, 17, 26; 3:5, 12, 21; 21:7; Mark 10:29–30; Luke 18:29–30.

Questions:

What are Jesus' promises to those who overcome?

_____

_____

_____

_____

Jesus promised provision for today to those who give their lives in service to Him. Do you experience that provision in your life? Why do you believe this is so?

_____

_____

_____

_____

In what ways do these provisions, both current and future, defeat the work of the enemy in your life?

_____

_____

_____

_____

How are these provisions appropriated?

_____

_____

_____

_____

Behind the Scenes

The enemy of God is our enemy. We are in a fight with a bully who has declared war on God and on us. He never gives up and, without the power of the blood activated in our lives, he never backs down.

In the invisible realm, a war is being fought between the angels of God and the fallen angels (those who follow and serve Satan). Although this war is taking place in an unseen dimension or spiritual world, it directly affects our present reality here on earth. Physical realities such as earthly governments, war, peace, revival, and evangelism are rooted in the spiritual activity of this invisible realm. This intense spiritual warfare is not only conducted by angelic forces, but is also waged here on the earth by believers who enter into militant, intercessory prayer. Through prayer, we are combatants in the struggle for the hearts and souls of humankind in the invisible realm. (Read Revelation 12:7–11.)

As people of the New Covenant, we have a job to do—a Great Commission to be lived (Matthew 28:18–20), a war to be waged, and a victory to be won. Anyone who has not yet known the salvation of God through the blood of Jesus is a prisoner of war to be rescued, for our Lord desires that all men come to a saving knowledge of Him (2 Peter 3:9). However, Jesus is our partner in the task and the battle; He has already won the victory over sin and death. He defeated Satan through the power of His cross. His victory is our victory and our triumph is assured through Him (1 Corinthians 15:57).

Kingdom Life—*Receive Power to Overcome*

The words "they overcame him by the blood of the Lamb" refer to the fact that the blood of Jesus Christ cleanses His church from the corrupting and contaminating power of sin. When this blood of the Lamb is appropriated by the people of God, a deep cleansing and purging of the death force is activated.

Jesus said, "He who believes in Me, as the Scripture has said, out of his heart will flow rivers of living water" (John 7:38). The blood of

Jesus Christ releases the blockage of sin inside of us so that Jesus' words can be fulfilled. His blood enables a divine release of the rivers of living water to flow unhindered from our inmost being. The surging stream of God's Spirit flowing from inside us drowns the flames of hell's fury in our lives and makes it possible for us to overcome Satan at every point.

It is the blood of Jesus Christ that makes possible the divine provision in Acts 1:8: "But you shall receive power when the Holy Spirit has come upon you; and you shall be witnesses to Me in Jerusalem, and in all Judea and Samaria, and to the end of the earth." The blood of Jesus Christ purifies us and redeems us so that God can pour out His Holy Spirit upon us.

This relationship between the blood of the Lamb and the release of the Spirit of God is a prime force in enabling us to overcome the power of the Devil.

Read Hebrews 2:14–15; 1 John 3:8.

Questions:

The fear of death, to which the verse in Hebrews refers, can have greater connotation than simple fear of physical death. What further meaning do you think can be applied here?

✎_____

_____

_____

How can these fears create a blockage within your life that inhibits the flow of God's Spirit?

✎_____

_____

How has the flow of God's Spirit enabled you to overcome Satan's schemes in your own life?

✎_____

_____

Kingdom Life—*No Condemnation*

As we learned in earlier lessons, Satan is the accuser of the brethren (Revelation 12:10) and there is a satanic strategy at work in attempting to destroy the word of our testimony and make us ineffective for Christ. Yet, through the powerful weapon of the blood of Christ, we can overcome Satan (Revelation 12:11).

Although Satan *can* accuse us, his accusations have no legal weight, because our righteousness is based in our being washed clean in the blood of the Lamb. Every time we make a mistake or sin, God erases that sin from the page of history when we confess our sin and are washed in the blood of the Lamb.

The great irony here is that it is Satan who tempts us to sin in the first place. Satan is the father of lies and a master trickster. He is the driving force behind all the wickedness in this world because this present world system is his doing. Yet if a Christian sins in thought, word, or deed, it is Satan—this totally impure and corrupt being and the father of this present sinful system—who dares to condemn the Christian and accuse him or her! However, the blood of Jesus Christ destroys the power of those accusations, because we are clean through the blood of Jesus Christ. In reality, our sins are not any of Satan's business because we are no longer his, but God's. We have been redeemed by the power of the blood.

Read John 1:29; 1 Corinthians 6:9–11; 2 Corinthians 7:10; Romans 8:1–11, 34–37, 1 John 1:8–9.

Questions:

What evidence do you see in your life that you have been "washed" and cleansed by the blood of Jesus?

_____

_____

_____

_____

What is the difference between godly sorrow and the condemnation sent by Satan?

_____

_____

_____

What affect does the condemnation of the enemy have on your life?

_____

_____

_____

What benefits are worked into your life through godly sorrow?

_____

_____

_____

Probing the Depths

Satan is our opponent, accuser, adversary, and enemy; he is the one who resists, obstructs, and hinders us. When people in our lives accuse, oppose, act as an adversary, resist, obstruct, hinder or, in general, play the role of an enemy, they are often motivated by Satan. In most cases, individuals being used by Satan are completely unaware of it. Their criticism of us may come from the merely human places of believing what they are doing is right; however, their opinions may have the deeper originations of jealousy, envy, or hatred. An individual or group, either Christian or non-Christian, can play this role. It makes no difference.

However, we must always remember that when God convicts us of sin, it is for the ultimate purpose of building us up. When Satan, through other people, condemns us, it leaves us feeling worthless, demoralized, and destroyed at some level. Often, it may be claimed that love is the motivation for hurtful and destructive words; but if motivated by love, they will have the end result of strengthening us and building us up.

All of us need to be accountable to brothers and sisters in Christ. Each of us needs constructive criticism in order to grow. God will use people in our lives (pastoral authority, elders, and mature members in the body of Christ) to shape and mold us. However, anyone who opposes us from self-centered motive, hates, obstructs, hinders what is good, or acts as an adversary or enemy is not from God. If the words spoken or written about us match up with the character of Satan, then it is extremely likely that Satan may be using someone to attack us.

We need discernment to know when God is correcting us and when Satan is attacking us.

Record Your Thoughts

The word of our testimony is that Jesus Christ is Lord and that He has defeated sin, death, and the powers of darkness on the Cross. Jesus Christ has been resurrected from the dead. This is a powerful testimony because it literally shatters the darkness of this present, satanic age and proclaims the light of the glory of the gospel of Jesus Christ. The supposed intellectual arguments of those embracing a humanistic world view come to nothing in light of Christ's resurrection from the dead. The historic proof of the resurrection of Jesus Christ echoes like a great sonic boom across the corridors of history, declaring the truth throughout the ages that Jesus Christ is Lord! Humanism becomes a moot point in light of the Resurrection. The teachings of men, such as Buddha and Muhammad, pale in comparison to the teachings of Jesus Christ, who proved His divinity by conquering death and rising from the dead. In fact, the actual resurrection of Jesus Christ from the dead makes Him completely unique among all men in history. The word of our testimony is that Jesus is Lord and He is alive, having been resurrected from the grave. The power of this truth has enabled Christians to stand before dictators and angry mobs, even to death.

Read Revelation 19:11—22:21.

As you consider the war in the heavenlies and the eventual, assured victory of the Lord, what affect should this inevitable outcome have on your daily life?

What can be the real-time affect on your life of continually recalling that the word of your testimony and the blood of Christ have defeated the power of sin?

At this point in our study, how do you now understand the designation People of the Covenant?

Conclusion

I f the Bible teaches us anything, especially as it relates to the great truths of the blood of the covenant and the Word of God, it teaches us that our universe is constructed according to spiritual laws and that these laws cannot be violated. The great mistake of our century is for modern man to attempt to analyze and understand physical, mathematical, and biological laws, while at the same time ignoring the spiritual laws of the universe. Just as the universe runs according to certain physical laws here on earth, such as the law of gravity, so the unseen dimension or the invisible realm functions according to specific laws. Thus, in man's dealings with God, we must comply with these laws. We simply cannot come to God or relate to Him in whatever way we choose. The entire fabric and construction of the universe hinges on the proper function-ing of spiritual law. God says that we must come to Him only through faith in Jesus Christ, which is an expression of the blood covenant, and that we must understand that God's Word is absolute. These are not just religious or whimsical beliefs that can be discarded carelessly. We must understand that at the very center of the universe, in the throne room of God, the Lamb sits upon the throne. In other words, ultimate reality is the very sum total and origination of all things that stem from a specific Supreme Being with a distinct divine personality transcendent of any human personality. Yet this Supreme Being lives in total harmony with the very universe He constructed and governs it according to His laws.

Therefore, when we glimpse into the Book of Revelation written by the apostle John on the Isle of Patmos, we are allowed to peer into heaven where we see the most awesome vision ever imaginable—a real-ity that is more real than the world we live in at this present moment (read Revelation 4:8–11). At the very center of the universe is the Lamb who sits upon the throne. The automatic response of the creation, when it is in right relationship with God and not deceived by the power of sin, is to worship the Lamb.

For a time, God has permitted humankind to rebel and erect a world system that is alien to His kingdom. However, this time period is drawing to a close as the end of history approaches. The sin that deceives humankind has been destroyed by the Lamb who has redeemed us by

His blood. In fact, at the very center of the universe is the final reality of the Lamb who exists, redeeming humankind by the blood. This is the very center of the universe and the very heartbeat of God reaching out in sacrificial love to men and women. What a marvelous truth that is! When we look up at the starry night sky and see the myriad display of lights twinkling in an infinite expanse, our hearts should rejoice because the universe is not empty, contrary to what the existentialists say. Nor is it a jungle where only the fittest survive. At the very center of the universe is a God of love, the Lamb upon the throne, who died so that you and I could have eternal life. Is it any wonder that part and parcel of this reality is a mighty song, a new song that gloriously proclaims the fact that the Lamb was slain for the sins of the world? He purchased eternal life for each of us by His blood. What other response can there be than a mighty, eternal anthem of praise and worship that fills the darkness of this present world with the splendor of His eternal glory as His life delivers us from darkness and floods our lives with the light of His life!

As the saints worship God and sing a new song, they are infused with the life of God Himself. Man becomes like what he worships. If a man worships money, sex, power and vanity, then he becomes a corrupt being, as empty as the object he worships. If men and women worship God, they become like the Lamb upon the throne and are filled with His presence.

The release of eternal life in our lives is made possible by the blood of the Lamb and the word of our testimony. When we are cleansed by the blood of the Lamb and are regenerated by the Word of God, the flow of God's life pours through us. God is life itself. He is the river of life (Revelation 22:1). The finished work on the Cross, the release of Christ's sacrificial blood, and the activation of the blood of the covenant through faith in the full authority of the Word of God allow the cleansing streams of heaven's glory to be poured through our lives.

This glory is released when we worship the Lamb upon the throne and sing a new song out of our inmost being. The worship of the Lamb upon the throne releases the presence of God in our midst. The blood of Jesus Christ paves the way for the release of this glory. This is how we overcome Satan by the word of our testimony and the blood of the Lamb. These two provisions make it possible for us to experience Revelation 22:1, not as just some far-off event, but as a present, moment-by-moment, experiential reality. The power of Satan is mortally crushed when the floodgates of God's river of glory are released in the lives of believers. The serpent of old, who deceived the human race in the Garden of Eden and who wages war against the saints, cannot withstand the fountains of glory that are released through praise and worship to the Lamb upon the throne!

As people of the covenant, let us stand strong in our faith with full assurance that our Lord has provided a way for us to know God and to come before His presence with confidence. We can stand before the very throne of grace and know the only true God because Jesus has provided the way—the new and living way.

ADDITIONAL OBSERVATIONS